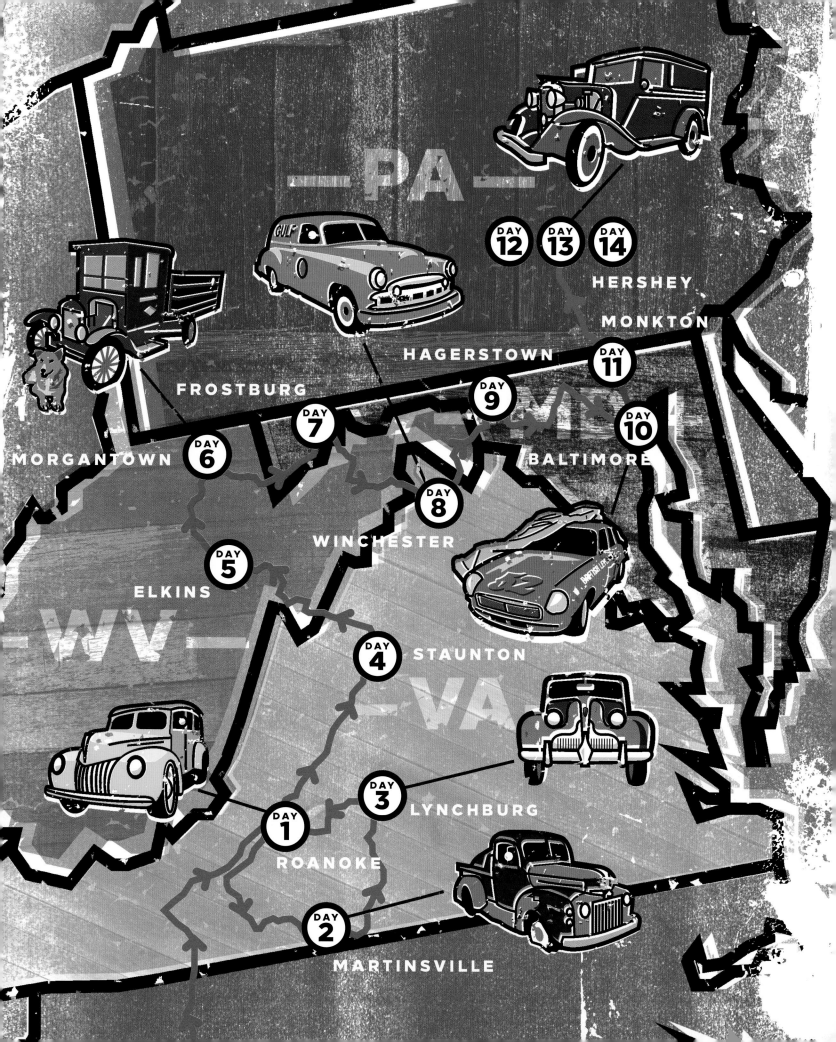

BARN FIND

Road Trip

TOM COTTER

— PHOTOGRAPHY BY —

MICHAEL ALAN ROSS

motorbooks

First published in 2015 by Motorbooks, an imprint of Quarto Publishing Group
USA Inc., 400 First Avenue North, Suite 400, Minneapolis, MN 55401 USA

Motorbooks titles are also available at discounts in bulk quantity for industrial
or sales-promotional use. For details write to Special Sales Manager at Quarto
Publishing Group USA Inc., 400 First Avenue North, Suite 400, Minneapolis, MN
55401 USA.

To find out more about our books, visit us online at www.motorbooks.com.

ISBN: 978-0-7603-4940-3

Acquisitions Editor: Zack Miller
Project Manager: Jordan Wiklund
Design Manager: Brad Springer
Cover Design: Kent Jensen
Layout Designer: Brad Norr Design

Printed in China

10 9 8 7 6 5 4 3 2 1

Dedication

To Peter Egan,
who unknowingly taught me everything I know about writing.
(Unfortunately, he failed to teach me everything *he* knew.)

ACKNOWLEDGMENTS

To my two car-hunting buddies—Brian Barr and Michael Alan Ross—who made this trip productive, memorable, and fun! To Zach Strait, who totally embraced the social media platform of our trip and guided us to a number of terrific discoveries in the central Virginia area. To friend Chuck Goldsborough, who not only turned us onto a number of really cool finds, but arranged for us to work on our disabled Woody in his brother's repair shop when we were stranded in the Baltimore area. To Keith Irwin and the guys at Keith Irwin Restorations, who have managed to keep the Woody roadworthy enough for our extended road trip. To the fine folks at Street and Performance, who are making good on the Woody's front belt drive system that gave us issues on our journey. To my Motorbooks publishing crew Zack Miller, Nichole (love the H) Schiele, Kathy Littfin, and Lara Neel, who wholeheartedly bought into the crazy concept of searching for cars and writing about it! And to my long-suffering wife, Pat, who had to do all the housework for two weeks.

Contents

Foreword

How many times have you driven down a country road and wondered what rare car or motorcycle was in the garage, barn, junkyard, or shed you just drove by? Lots of times, I bet. Tom Cotter, through his series of books, *The Cobra in the Barn, The Hemi in the Barn, The Vincent in the Barn,* and *50 Shades of Rust,* has given us a peek into garages, barns, junkyards, and even a bedroom (easy now, it was Henry Wilkinson's Cobra), supporting that dream we all have of finding the car we've always wanted and at a price we could afford.

All of the following stories were collected through Tom's myriad contacts, rumors, and whispers, but now he and his cohorts have taken it to a new level. Driving his '39 Ford Woody (a barn find itself) on a 2,700-mile odyssey through Virginia, West Virginia, Maryland, and Pennsylvania—and without the benefit of a television production company choreographing the trip—they dropped in on likely candidates. Taking the Woody was a good idea, as it was a great icebreaker and I am sure kept the guys from getting shot nosing around somebody's premises.

Tom, along with Brian Barr and ace photographer Michael Alan Ross, found a treasure trove of Chevys, Fords, a Cord Beverly sedan…hey! Read the book. They are all here. And the guys did it the old-fashioned way: cruising the highways and byways and just following their noses.

Maybe this book will influence you to hit the road with the same goal. If you don't, Tom will beat you to that lost Cobra, Ferrari, Duesenberg, or Bugatti. To quote the ever erudite Bluto from *Animal House,* you know what this means—*ROAD TRIP!* Enjoy the ride and savor the dream.

Bill Warner
Founder and Chairman
Amelia Island Concours d'Elegance

Introduction

—— BEST ROAD TRIP EVER ——

For adult males of the gear-head persuasion, discovering an old car is a very special occasion. I say male because I have not met too many women who get their jollies by digging through mechanical trash, sneaking into barns and outbuildings, or risking tick and snake bites in the hopes of finding a vintage vehicle. But for certain guys, an environment like this is utopia.

Perhaps there is an endorphin release, similar to the "high" that distance runners experience when going on a long run. For hard-core, truly addicted barn-finders, "the search" is at least as exciting as "the find," and many times more so. As my friend Peter Egan says regarding intensive automotive restoration, "It's about the journey, not the destination." After years of wrenching to complete a restoration, enthusiasts like Peter simply sell the car into which they have invested so much blood, sweat, and tears—and simply purchase another project.

Peter wrote this in the Foreword of *The Cobra in the Barn*, my first book on this subject: "Finding that car in a barn and making it run again are as close as most car buffs will ever get to God."

Well said.

For serious car finders, it's much the same way. The simple task of following up on obscure leads that "might" yield a car is reason enough to waste away a perfectly good Saturday. And actually finding the car is gear-head nirvana.

I speak as one of the thoroughly addicted. Since way before I actually held a driver's license, I have been searching for old cars. Perhaps it was because I showed no interest (or ability) in organized sports or education; from grade school through high school I was more absorbed in reading my favorite monthly magazine, *Rod & Custom*, than in academics or throwing a perfect pitch. *Rod & Custom* featured a regular column entitled

10,000 PHOTOS LATER

I've been very lucky in my life. As an automotive photographer, I've had the pleasure of working with some of the most amazing, talented individuals.

The greatest thing about this journey has been the people—the ones who create and sweat over their passion. The designers, journalists, photographers, collectors, and of course the enthusiasts who spend hours reading magazines or leaning over the fence at the racetrack; we are all connected.

That is why I said yes to Tom Cotter's crazy idea about doing a 14-day road trip in search of barn finds. Besides, rust *is* the new chrome.

The next thing I knew, I was standing in a field of rusty Ford Galaxies. We drove thousands of miles, documenting cars and making new friends along the way.

We saw way more than we could ever fit in this book, and God knows there are a few stories that will remain between Tom, Brian, and me.

I saw, sat in, bumped up against, and stepped in things I never thought would be associated with an automobile shoot. Would I do it again? In a heartbeat. It's experiences like these that ground and connect you to what automobiles and friendship are all about.

A barn find is more than just an abandoned car. It's a story of who owned it, how it got there, and why it's still there. I encourage you to go take a road trip with a few friends. You never know what you'll find.

Michael Alan Ross

"Vintage Tin." This column showed photos of old cars, perfect hot-rod material, usually in deserted locations. Ford roasters, T-buckets, Woody wagons and pickups, all looking slightly weathered, were featured in black-and-white photos. I just knew some lucky California hot rodder would purchase one and embark on a cool project.

Living on the East Coast, I felt denied of that experience, so I started searching for old cars in my region. I often looked out the school-bus window or rode my bicycle up and down neighborhood streets, looking for interesting tin.

During my first two years of high school, I went to a Catholic school, Seton Hall, in Patchogue, New York. My friend, Xavier Lucena—a fellow car guy—and I would walk the streets of Patchogue after school. Dressed in our school's blue blazers and ties, we knocked on

doors, asking about old cars in people's backyards. And we found a bunch; this was 45 years ago, but I still remember a blue 1940 Mercury coupe, a black 1946–48 Ford convertible, a black '36 Ford sedan, and a bunch of Model As.

When I was old enough for a driver's license, my friends Phil Braddock, Vinnie Maggio, Tommy Allen, and I would occasionally cut class and travel to Long Island's east end in search of old cars. My personal interest lay in 1935 to 1940 Fords, because I liked their round body styles. But Phil preferred earlier, more angular-styled cars—Model Ts and Model As, which he called "Squares."

I remember once Phil hollered, "Square," as we drove by a farm, and what he thought was an early-model car parked next to a barn; it actually turned out to be an outhouse that somehow resembled a Model T coupe.

Today, being a longtime member of the Early Ford V-8 Club of America, my favorite column in the *V-8 Times* magazine is "They're Still Out There," which features photos of old flathead-powered Fords that still languish behind buildings and in fields today.

Which is the purpose of this book.

People comment to me all the time that there are no old cars remaining; that they were all discovered 10 or 20 years ago. Baloney, I say. I can't drive to the local pizza place without finding an interesting vehicle.

After an all-day trial run with my good friend, Brian Barr—where we discovered at least 10 great vehicles in Western North Carolina—I called my publisher at Motorbooks, Zack Miller, and told him that I thought I had an idea for a new book. A true "reality" book.

All the "amazing" discoveries you see on the popular TV programs are really not too amazing after all. They have all been thoroughly vetted by producers, weeks before the camera crews arrive. It's all carefully choreographed, with lighting and sound engineers all in place.

I told Zack, "I'd like to write a book based on discovering cars the old-fashioned way: going down interesting roads and knocking on doors."

The working title of this book was *Barn Find Road Trip: 3 Guys, 14 Days, 100 Cars.*

"Do you think you can find 100 cars?" he asked.

"I think so," I told him. "But it's really hard to predict." Convinced we had a decent idea, he gave us the go-ahead to spend 14 days documenting our discoveries.

Enjoy the next 14 chapters, one for each day. Some days were more prosperous than others, but every day was memorable.

And remember, "They're still out there!"

Tom Cotter

—— A LIFETIME FULFILLED ——

I've always said my headstone will read, "Here lies Brian Barr. Racer, Writer, Rocker." While I have raced in amateur and vintage events and played in a rock band (35 years ago), I wasn't sure how I would fulfill the "writer" epitaph. Thanks to Tom Cotter, I was invited to participate in this fantastic adventure and book. In writing this, I'd say that's close enough!

Growing up in New York, I was always California dreaming. I discovered hot rods and sports cars along the way. My dad was a car guy and DIY mechanic. I was his willing assistant. Both my grandfathers taught me the skills of car hunting. They were always searching for old iron when poking around town or traveling across the countryside. I enjoyed riding with them and hearing their stories.

When Tom invited me to participate in this epic adventure, I jumped at the chance. I spent two weeks poking though hidden treasure and anticipating the next one with a couple of great guys. We talked cars 24/7. We met interesting people. With every turn there was excitement and anticipation. This is what cars do; they are more than transportation. Cars are time machines, memory makers, and rolling art, especially when viewed through the lens of Michael Alan Ross.

Tom is a great friend. We never run out of car stories to talk about, and it seems we haven't run out of cars to find either.

Thank you Tom, Michael, and all the new friends we met along the way!

Brian Barr

A Brief Note About the Stories in Barn Find Road Trip

Cars featured in this book might have been for sale when I wrote it in the fall of 2014. These for-sale references were meant to be interesting tidbits about how many cars are actually still out there and available for purchase. I am not suggesting, however, that these cars are still available, and I am not acting as a broker for the owners.

If you are interested in pursuing the purchase of any of these cars, do not contact me. If you decide to pursue any of the cars in this book, there are enough clues to make it possible.

Thank you for your consideration.

DAY

I had a bagel with chicken salad and a Snapple Iced Tea at Bagel Bin in Huntersville, North Carolina. I'm watching my calorie intake, so I bypassed the potato chips. My two traveling companions, Brian Barr and Michael Alan Ross, had similar sandwiches, which, we surmised, would give us the energy for the tough journey on which we were about to embark.

It was noontime on Friday, September 26, and we had been challenged by Motorbooks to find and document all the old cars we could in 14 days. We felt up to the task, but decided to start our adventure with full stomachs.

We decided to budget our time in four states, spending between three and four days each in Virginia, West Virginia, Maryland, and Pennsylvania. We planned to end our trip at the Hershey, Pennsylvania, Antique Car Club of America (AACA) swap meet and car show.

In the parking lot were the two vehicles we would navigate for the next couple of weeks: my 1939 Ford Woody wagon and a 2014 Ford Flex. Brian and I, the two certified barn-find geeks, would drive the Woody. Michael, my photographer friend, would drive the Flex that was kindly loaned to us by Ford Motor Company. I had the pleasure of working with Michael in the past on the book *Rockin' Garages*, co-authored by Ken Gross and me.

The Woody would be our lead car, our rolling billboard, so-to-speak, and the Flex would contain all Michael's photography equipment and our suitcases. With a full tank of fuel, the Woody had 21,806 miles on the odometer when we departed.

Which way would we go? Didn't know, but we knew two things: I didn't want to search for old cars in North Carolina because I didn't want the potential criticism of "discovering" cars I might have already known about in my home state, and I wanted our tour to end at the AACA flea market two weeks later. Other than that, all bets were off.

(top) The Three Amigos—Michael Alan Ross, Brian Barr, and Tom Cotter—with our *Barn Find Road Trip* vehicles, the 1939 Ford Woody, and the 2014 Ford Flex, moments before leaving Cotter's driveway for the 14-day adventure.

(left) My publisher had these decals made for the side windows of the Woody, and we had miniature versions of the decals that we gave out to interested people en route.

So after we ate our hearty sandwiches, drank our beverages, and said goodbye to the girls behind the counter, we climbed into our vehicles and headed north on Interstate 77. I knew we could be in Virginia in about an hour, and this way we could begin our car hunting adventures sometime in the early to mid-afternoon time frame, rather than just use Friday as a commuting day.

It was a glorious day as we traveled north past Statesville, Harmony, and Mt. Airy. In about one hour, we crossed the North Carolina—Virginia state line at a wonderfully scenic region called Fancy Gap. When our country's founders were designing the state boundaries, they obviously decided that the flat land would become North Carolina and the mountainous area would be Virginia. This is very unlike the Four Corners National Monument out west; Virginia's southern border and North Carolina's northern border is that clear.

Another 30 minutes north, as we were approaching the intersection of I-77 and I-81, Brian and I both shouted at the same moment: "CARS!"

Our Woody veered sharply to the right, with Michael in the Flex following (sorry for the radical move, Mikey...) We both parked, probably illegally, on the shoulder of the highway as cars and trucks passed mere feet away at 80 miles per hour. I didn't know if what we were doing was illegal, but it certainly was unsafe. Nonetheless, we were on a mission to discover old cars, and this was our first find.

There, on the east side of the interstate, off in the distance, was a field of steel. Some of it was shiny, some of it dull, but all of it rusty. We used my small binoculars, but then Brian got a little bit fancy.

"Watch this," said our expedition's techno-genius, as he fiddled with his iPhone. After a couple of minutes, he showed Michael and me his screen. "I figured we'd try Google Earth!"

So, we were looking at a field of vintage cars, assisted by a satellite camera located several hundred miles above us in space. I was amazed. And glad Brian was so technically savvy. Then, for a better view, Michael installed his telephoto lens and confirmed that the cars in the field were, indeed, vintage tin.

We needed to find a road to that field. So Brian secured the satellite location of the field, then he pinned it on his GPS so we could locate it from the other

direction. We climbed back into our cars and continued north on I-77 and took the very next exit onto I-81 North. We took the first exit off I-81 and figured the field of cars couldn't be too far away.

Soon after exiting the highway, we came across a terrific series of old mill buildings. We had to stop. Here were a bunch of buildings that had obviously been vacant for many years. A man who passed by in a pickup truck stopped and told us it had once been a grain mill and general store. It resembled an abandoned Western town.

We wanted to climb the fence and explore inside, but decided to respect the No Trespassing sign. We admired a rusty old gas pump next to the general store. I imagine that before I-81 was constructed, this might have been a popular area for locals to shop. But we had cars to find, and we needed to keep moving in the direction of those cars in the field. On we drove.

The pavement eventually ran out, and we continued on a dusty gravel road. I had just washed and waxed the Woody a few hours earlier, so this dust was making me slightly depressed. After rounding a few corners, and going over a few hills, we arrived at a location that Brian said was "The Place."

There was no mistaking it; under a carport on the left side of the road, were two Ford Galaxies, a 1964 and a 1965, in various stages of disassembly and/or restoration. To the right of the road were a few barns with various 1960s Fords scattered about.

We parked the cars. I walked up to the house adjacent to the carport and knocked on the door. A burley man came to the door and smiled. I was instantly relieved. "I saw your Woody drive up," he said. "I'd like to take a look at it." We shook hands. The man introduced himself as Snowball Bishop, and he was instantly our friend.

Clearly, Snowball Bishop—don't you just love his name—has been into cars his whole life.

SNOWBALL BISHOP'S FIELD OF FORDS

Car Count	For Sale?		
approx **60**	YES	NO	MAYBE

"Brother, at one time I had 17 1940 Ford coupes," he said. "I'd make race cars out of them. Right now all I got are these old Fords here, some in the other building and in the field, and I got the old race car in the other shop."

I quickly realized that our visit to Snowball's house was not going to be a short one. I told Snowball, "We saw your field from the interstate." He told us that sometimes folks see his cars from the highway and just climb over the fence and walk on in, leaving their cars sitting on the interstate!

"I'm 85-years-old, brother," he said. "I've been collecting cars my whole life."

Snowball invited us into one of his garages to see a couple of his favorite cars. He was obviously a Ford man, and, as we would discover, an enthusiast of the 390-cubic-inch FE engine. He lifted up the car cover and revealed a pristine, white 1964 Ford two-door hardtop.

"This one has a 390 in it with 300 horsepower," said Snowball. "I've had this one since 1968."

He led us to another covered car in the garage. As he lifted the cover, it revealed another 1964 Ford, this time a brilliant blue Galaxie. I jokingly asked him, "Is 1964 the year you were born?" He laughed and said he wished that were the case.

"Now this one here, I tore all the way [apart] about 15 years ago," he said. "This one here is a 390, four-speed car. I didn't like

On the way to Snowball's in Virginia, we came upon this long-closed general store and grain mill. We wanted to explore it, but decided to respect the No Trespassing sign.

the factory metallic blue, so I changed it to this color. I restored this one myself."

I asked him about the cars in the field behind his barn. "Are those cars all parts cars?"

"A lot of them are parts car, but some of them out there can be put back on their feet," he said. "I brought in another 1963 and a 1964 just the other day. And I bought a 1963 convertible that some other boy started on, but cancer got him, so I bought it."

Then he pointed to a 1965 Ford his son had recently dragged home.

"It's a 1965 Ford that had been put up 18 years ago," he said. "It's got a solid body on it, and it's a 390 car. The frame is good under it. It had no engine in it, so [the owner] started out wanting $2,000 for the car. My son Jimmy offered him $1,500 for the car, and he took it home."

Then Snowball showed us some photos of himself as a younger man.

"Is that you?" Brian asked.

"Yes, that's me when I was racing," he said. "I have a whole house full of them [photos]."

Not now, Brian! We have cars to find!

We parked the Woody in front of Snowball Bishop's garage for the first barn find of our adventure, just 90 minutes into our trip!

Modified Racer

Apparently, Snowball had been quite a driver on the NASCAR Modified circuit back in the day.

"I've got my old '37 Ford race car in the other garage. Would you like to see it?" I thought Brian was going to burst at the seams with excitement.

As we walked toward the garage, Snowball got reminiscent. "Now this place here has a lot of history," he said. "I think Daddy put this building up in the 1950s. At the time, it was all we had. We didn't have any money back then. It's a wonder that this old building hasn't burned up three or four times. We used to heat it with an old pot-belly stove that was in the corner.

Snowball Bishop has an amazing life story. Since his wife passed away a decade ago, car people have become his family.

The only power we had was to run a power cord from our house across the street."

As he opened the door, sunlight shone on the race car that had been a part of his life for so many years. "One time when we rebuilt that old car, we put a Chevy frame under it," he said.

I asked when he purchased the car. He said it was so long ago he couldn't remember. "I had so many coupes back then, I don't know when I bought this one. But if I'm not mistaken, I think I got this car from the Jackson boys. I think the last time I raced it was in 1973 or 1974, I can't remember."

Snowball said that he built the coupe in this very garage.

"Did it race with a Ford engine?" I asked?

Snowball told us he initially raced with a series of modified flathead engines and usually finished in the top five against the more modern overhead-valve Chevy engines in the 1960s. He talks proudly of a couple of Crossfire flatheads he ran. Crossfire engines fire two sparkplugs at once. After flatheads, he tried a Holman-Moody-built 312 cubic-inch engine, then a 406 cubic-inch Ford, but ultimately decided to switch to Mopar

Snowball uncovers a '64 Galaxie, this one powered by a 390 and a four-speed. He restored this car about 15 years ago, and decided to change the color to metallic blue. He also owns a '66 Galaxie two-door hardtop.

I thought Brian was going to burst! Snowball led us into his "race barn" to show us the 1937 Modified racer he drove until the mid-1970s.

engines. In later years, the car ran with a 413-cubic-inch Chrysler engine with a four-speed gearbox, but that changed when he bought a load of engines and parts from Petty Enterprises.

Petty Connection

"I'm telling you the honest truth," said Snowball. "I drove up to Richard Petty's house with my old pickup, and maybe I had $1,000 in my pocket. Old man Lee Petty was sitting there in a chair and said, 'How are you boys getting along?'

"'Mr. Lee,' I said. 'I heard you were selling some good 426 stuff, and we're here to buy it. We're looking for the good Stage 3 heads and the good intakes. My 413 runs good, but it won't beat the Chevys anymore.'

"Lee said, 'See that pile of stuff there in the corner? There's three engines there and enough parts to build two more. If I'm not mistaken, there are six Stage 3 heads in there, and all sorts of camshafts, pistons, rods.'

This is a barn-find scene that dreams are made of! Snowball's '37 Ford Modified car is an authentic racer that has had an amazing career on tracks throughout Virginia and North Carolina.

"Richard had gone to the Hemi engine by then, so he was selling all the 426 Wedge stuff," said Snowball. "So Lee says, 'What would you give me for it? Would you give $1,000 for all that stuff in the corner?' I said, 'Mr. Lee, you wouldn't lower that just a little so I have enough money to get home, would you?' He died laughing and took $900 for everything.

"Later I ran a 440-cubic-inch Chrysler engine in the car," he said. "The engine for it is out of it now and is sitting next to it on the floor. I turn it over every week."

Before we left the old garage, Snowball told us that, besides working on the old stock car, he also used the garage as a makeshift poker parlor.

"We'd start playing cards, and about one or two o'clock in the morning, my wife would start cutting out the lights by pulling the power cord out of the socket up at the house. That was the time to go on home. Those were the good old days."

The Coupe Today

"I don't want to put the motor back in it until the car is painted," he said. "I told Jimmy, 'Hey, you better get on the ball and get this thing painted. Daddy might not

Snowball is contemplating whether to restore his old coupe, which is built on a Chevy chassis and has a 440 Mopar engine. He built this car in this very garage 50 years ago.

be here too much longer. I'd like to hear that thing run again.' You wouldn't believe how many people tried to buy that old car off of me. Ray Evernham wanted to buy it."

As we walked to his other garage, Snowball said that when I-77 was built, it cut his farm in two. He said he still owns about 100 acres of land on one side, and about 39 acres on the side where his home and cars sit.

Snowball's father had scrimped and saved and bought the farm back in the 1930s during the Depression. He explained that he and his siblings were raised in the family's old home place at the lower end of the field. There used to be an old schoolhouse on the property that his mother attended.

Snowball said he acquired an additional 2-acre lot below the family property years ago, which is where he used to keep his cars. "I used to keep that lot plum full of old cars; I had 1937, '39, '40 Fords up in there and plum up into the 1950s, coupes, pickups. I just phased them out; people bought them up, and I couldn't find no more.

As we walked past my Woody, he stopped to admire it. I told him I bought it in 1969 when I was 15 years old. He wanted to look under the hood, but I told him I didn't want to ruin his day.

"You have a Chevy in there, don't you?" he asked as I reached for the hood latch.

"Yes I do," I said. "Even though I'm a Ford guy, I couldn't say no to this LS1 engine."

"Mmmmmm, mmmmm, that sure is sweet," he said.

The next garage, like the previous one, was loaded with 1963 and 1964 Ford pieces: grilles, trim, emblems, headlight doors. "I've got a field full of 1964 Fords. And that old house over there is filled with parts and junk, Lord have mercy."

Huge 1963 and '64 Ford Stash

"You wouldn't believe that they come from everywhere looking for 1963 and 1964 Ford stuff off of me," said Snowball. "They'll stop over there on the interstate and walk across the pasture to find me. They'll say, 'We didn't know how to get here.'

"I sell the boys some things, because you can't find these old parts anymore. I've sold Larry McClure a lot of stuff over the years. He's the boy who owned the [NASCAR] team that Sterling Marlin and Ernie Irvan drove for. He has some old Fords and was restoring some old Galaxies back. He called me the other day and was looking for a console and a set of bucket seats for an XL.

"I sell cars and parts when I can. I try to help the boys out. If I got it, I'll let you have it. If I don't have it, they'll just have to go on down the road to someone else."

We walked toward a newer, steel building. Snowball said that he recently had it constructed for some of his nicer cars.

As we raised the door, our eyes instantly went toward a beautiful 1963 Ford Galaxie convertible.

"It came from North Wilkesboro," said Snowball. "I guess I'm the second owner on it. Everybody who sees this sharp old '63 wants to buy it. It is a factory four- speed car, and it is unrestored.

"I bought it about five years ago. I bought it from a boy named Jimmy Williams who had a stroke, and because it's a four-speed car, he couldn't shift it anymore, so I went over and bought it from him."

Then Snowball told us we could walk down into the field and look at his other cars.

(above) Snowball's son recently dragged home this 1965 Ford Galaxie. He paid $1,500 and hopes to restore the car, which was originally powered by a 390.

(below) Talk about a big powerplant! Obviously this 1964 Ford has been parked in Snowball's field for a long, long time.

—— FORDS IN THE FIELD ——

"There's a landmark out there," he said. "It's a 1964 XL that was parked there in 1972 or 1973. It's a tree car!" There was a mature tree coming out of where the engine used to be! Talk about a power plant…

Before we said goodbye, I took my notepad and made a count of just how many cars Snowball had in total, in his garages and in the field. I might have missed one or two, but it breaks down this way: there's his 1937 Ford modified car, a 1957 Ford, 16 1963 Fords, 26 1964 Fords, 3 1965 Fords, 2 1963 or 64 Mercury Montereys, 2 1966-ish Ford Thunderbirds, and a few other non-Fords scattered about.

That totals about 60 cars. When I told Snowball the number, he said: "I had over 100 at one time."

Obviously this '64 Ford hasn't been parked for quite as long as the other. A smaller tree seems to be coming out of where the four-barrel carburetor would rest.

You say you need a hubcap? Snowball has stacks of them for many 1960s and 1970s Fords.

A Mercury sandwich. This 1963 Mercury Monterrey two-door is surrounded by a pair of 1963 Fords on the left, and a pair of 1964 Fords on the right.

This 1959 Ford two-door sedan already has had some parts removed from it, including the rear end.

Brian (right) helps Snowball uncover the 1964 Ford Galaxie two-door hardtop he has owned since 1968. The car has a 390-cubic-inch engine with an automatic.

— BACK ON THE ROAD —

After a couple of pleasant hours visiting Snowball, we said goodbye and continued northbound. We couldn't have been much luckier on the first of our 14-day tour than to discover this many cars just 90 minutes after leaving Bagel Bin! How many other Snowball Bishops would we be lucky enough to meet over the next two weeks?

We decided that Roanoke, Virginia, would be a good stopping point for the night, so we headed north in that direction. And, since it was Friday, we hoped we could locate an evening cruise-in and get some leads on old cars that could be followed up the next day.

We asked around and found out there was a weekly cruise-in at the Lowe's shopping center. So that's where we headed. We pulled into the Lowe's parking lot. Only a couple of dozen cool cars were present, mostly Chevelles and Novas, but also a couple contemporaries of my Woody. The three of us dispersed quickly and began telling people of our mission.

After leaving Snowball's, we headed north and located this cruise-in in a Roanoke-area Lowe's store. The leads we had hoped to gather, though, never materialized.

We began an almost nightly ritual of visiting local pubs. This was our first, the Wasena City Brewing Company, in Roanoke.

"We're looking for old cars," we said. "Do you have any, or know of anybody who has old cars?"

We about blanked out. Not much response. These guys had cool cars, but they didn't keep old parts cars around their houses. All they knew about barn finds were what they saw on TV. What was the matter with them?

I surmised that these were nouveau car guys: recently retired gentlemen who had spare cash and bought cars they had admired earlier in their lives. But they were not organic "greasy finger" car guys; I call them "fluffers and buffers."

I was beginning to get depressed until one gentleman said he knew of an old Plymouth Superbird sitting at a house a few exits south off I-81. He gave us a few vague directions. Hmmm, vague directions often become dead ends, I thought. But I filed it in my brain's hard drive and said thank you.

We also heard about a place called British Auto Restorations in Roanoke, but they were closed on the weekends, so we promised to search for it next week.

Tomorrow was another day.

ALL MAKES, MODELS, AND STORIES CONSIDERED

What is a cool car? As we drove around for the next couple of weeks, we would be looking for cool cars, but what qualified as a cool car?

Basically, I was able to play God, because I determined what ultimately went into this book. To put it simply, no K cars! Sorry, but I don't care for K cars, or any of the K car's variants, even the rare turbocharged convertibles with fake wood siding.

And no GM front-wheel-drive cars that were manufactured in the 1980s, cars like the terrible Citation. I'll never forget when Chevy used the national 55-miles-per-hour speed limit as an excuse to install weaker (cheaper) "55-mile-per-hour" brakes in the Citation and other GM cars of the era. I haven't thought much about those cars since.

Other than that, every vehicle built before World War II, as well as post–World War II through the 1970s, would be fair game. And, selectively, I would consider cars built after that. But into the 1980s and beyond, my interest falls off pretty rapidly. Of course there were great cars built during that era, but they were not right for this book.

Other than that, foreign and domestic cars, trucks, motorcycles, sports cars, and four-door sedans, and perhaps even heavy equipment. It's good to be the barn-find God!

DAY

*R*eflecting back on our first half-day on the road, we certainly couldn't have hoped for much better. We left my home at noon, just hoping to get out of North Carolina and begin our car search the next day. The fact that we actually discovered old cars just 90 minutes into our trip was certainly a positive step. That the find was Snowball Bishop's stash of 60-something cars was amazing.

We were on a high, and couldn't wait to see what today, a beautiful Saturday morning, would bring.

En route to Roanoke, we stopped for fuel in Salem, Virginia, and the Woody took 10.4 gallons of 93 octane. We had driven 239 miles on Day 1, and the 75-year-old car with the late model drivetrain got almost 24 miles per gallon!

The night before at the cruise-in, we were told of a car show that would be held this morning in the parking lot of the nearby Tanglewood Shopping Mall. We figured that would be great place to start, so we headed there first thing.

The show was smaller than I had hoped, mostly populated by Pontiacs. We saw some beautiful GTOs, Firebirds, and the like, but there were no barn finds to be found. I walked over to registration table and asked some of the gentlemen in charge if they knew of any old cars around.

I got pretty much the same answers as the night before; they talked about the TV shows they had seen, but nobody seemed to know of any barn finds in the area. It's as if finding barn-find cars is a Hollywood phenomenon, and that these opportunities don't exist in real life. I felt like shouting, "They are all around you, folks," but held my tongue.

Then Kenny Dancy, one of the men at the registration table, mentioned that he had recently purchased an old car near his home near Wytheville, Virginia: a 1948 Chevrolet sedan delivery.

"I bought it from my next-door neighbor, who has lots of old cars hidden in the bamboo," he said.

Carmike Cinemas

1	MAZE RUNNER
2	WALK AMONG THE TOMBSTONES
3	BOX TROLLS NOVEMBER MAN
4	IF I STAY
5	NO GOOD DEED
6	EQUALIZER
7	THIS IS WHERE I LEAVE YOU
8	DOLPHINS TALE 2
9	GUARDIANS OF GALAXY
10	

(top) On the morning of Day 2, we attended a shopping mall car show sponsored by the Pontiac Club. We got blank stares when we asked where we could locate some barn finds. Again.

(left) Even though we had washed the Woody the day before, we couldn't say no to this charity car wash in the mall parking lot to benefit juvenile diabetes research.

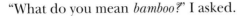

"What do you mean *bamboo?*" I asked.

"Yes, the cars have been parked there so long, a bamboo forest has grown around them," he said. "I need to go in there with a machete and cut my car out."

I said we were heading north, but that perhaps we would stop by his house near the end of our two-week trip. We shook hands and said goodbye. Interestingly, this would not be the last time we would experience cars hidden in a bamboo forest during this trip. More on that later.

Anyway, we weren't getting anywhere at the car show, so we decided to follow up on the lead we received the night before about the Plymouth Superbird south of Roanoke.

It was already 1:00 p.m. on Saturday afternoon as we drove toward the supposed Superbird, and we had not yet found a single barn find. This was depressing, because just 24 hours earlier, we had discovered Snowball's collection of old Fords just 90 minutes into our trip, and today we had already spent 4 hours looking and talking with car people and still hadn't turned up a single lead. Perhaps we had been spoiled on our first day and would never experience that type of discovery again.

Little did we know that our luck was about to turn around.

We were told the Plymouth was near an interstate exit with a heavy equipment dealer on the corner. We drove to that exit, and son-of-a-gun, there was the equipment dealer.

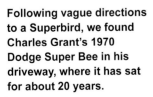

Following vague directions to a Superbird, we found Charles Grant's 1970 Dodge Super Bee in his driveway, where it has sat for about 20 years.

So far, so good.

We turned right, as instructed, and drove about a half-mile to the end of the road. And there, in a front yard, was not actually a Plymouth Superbird, but a Dodge Super Bee! No wings and pointy noses, but still a pretty cool discovery.

The tip turned out to be a good one.

CHARLES GRANT'S 1970 DODGE SUPER BEE

Car Count	For Sale?		
4	YES	NO	MAYBE

I knocked on the door, and a woman answered. I told her I was writing a book about old cars and would like to discuss the Dodge in her driveway.

"I'll call my husband," she said. Her name was Gloria. "He's working on the roof around back."

Within a few minutes, we were talking with the Super Bee's owner, Charles Grant, who had bought the car new!

"I bought it right here in Salem in 1970," said Charles. "I traded in a 1964 Ford Galaxie XL500 with a 390-cubic-inch plus about $4,000 for the car."

Charles' Super Bee has a 383-cubic-inch engine with a four-barrel carb and automatic transmission. Sitting there in his yard, the odometer registers 142,000 miles. It was last registered in 1996. So it's been sitting idle for 18 years.

"I saw that car at three o'clock in the morning on the dealer lot, so about a week later I went back and bought it," he said.

When the car was new, it was red with a white vinyl roof and a reflective C-stripe along the side. Over the years, Charles had it repainted orange after it was involved in a minor collision. Charles told me that even though the car has the original rally wheels on it, at one time he ran chrome rims with

Charles' Super Bee is powered by a potent 383-cubic-inch with a four-barrel with 142,000 miles on it. The car was last registered in 1996.

10-inch slicks on the back. I asked Charles if he had ever drag raced the car? No. Had he ever street raced it? No.

"How fast have you had the car up to," I asked.

"I've had it up to 120 miles-per-hour," he said. "But it gets light in the front end when you go that fast. And the drum brakes are not the best."

I asked if he was going to restore the Super Bee.

"At 68 years old, I'm not sure I'm going to do anything with it, but my son is chomping at the bit for it," he said. "I just haven't decided to give it to him yet."

Charles bought this car new off the local Dodge dealership in Salem, Virginia. He admits to driving the car to 120 miles per hour "before the front end got light."

Charles said he had a couple of other old vehicles, like a 1956 Dodge ¾-ton truck his father bought from the original owner. The truck now belongs to Charles Grant Jr., Charles' son. Interestingly, Charles was driving this very truck the night he saw and fell in love with his Super Bee in 1970. The truck reminded me of what Timmy's father drove on the Lassie TV program.

He also showed us a couple of cars his younger brother owns, one he thinks is a 1967 Dodge Coronet R/T with a 400-cubic-inch, last driven in 1985, the other a Chevelle two-door hidden in the woods.

After leaving Charles and his Super Bee, we decided to head south on less-traveled roads, specifically Highway 11, which was once a main north-south thoroughfare before the interstate was installed. We soon passed an old commercial garage that didn't appear to be in business. We stopped because we noticed several old pickup trucks behind the building. Brian and I peeked

This is the 1956 Dodge ¾-ton pickup that Charles was driving the night he saw his Super Bee parked on the dealer's lot in 1970. Today the truck sits in a field near his house.

into one of the garage doors, and there was a partially disassembled 1937 Ford two-door sedan. But nobody was around, and there was no phone number on the building, so we kept driving.

A little further down the road, we came across a used-car dealer that specialized in muscle cars. We figured they might know if there were any old cars in the area, but when we walked inside the showroom, nobody was there. We walked back into the shop, but there was nobody there, either.

Hmmm. A dozen pristine old cars sat in the showroom. The lights and radio were on, but nobody was around. We figured that whoever was there that Saturday afternoon was probably out test-driving a car that he had been working on.

As we were leaving, a woman drove up and asked if we worked at the dealership. We said no. Then she said, "Well, I'd like to sell my 1963½ Ford Falcon convertible I have at home, and wanted to see if this dealership would like to buy it."

I asked what condition the Falcon was in, and she said perfect.

"My husband just had it restored last year."

I told her we were on the road to discover barn finds, not perfectly restored cars, so we said goodbye and continued on our way.

Charles' younger brother owns this 1967 Dodge Coronet R/T, last registered in 1985. The car has a 400-cubic-inch and a floor-mounted automatic shifter.

Charles' brother also had this 1966 Malibu sitting behind the house.

— NOBODY HOME —

It's so frustrating to come across a potential gold mine of old cars but find nobody around. Such was the case with B&M Motors in Christiansburg, Virginia. It had obviously been a repair shop or a junkyard, but certainly had been out of business for many years.

There were a number of cars littered about, including a 1951 or '52 Chrysler two-door, but nobody was there, and the place was plastered with Private Property and No Trespassing signs. We decided to stay on the right side of the law and continue driving down the road rather than climb over the fence.

Another side-of-the-road discovery was a decent 1957 Chevy sedan that was stored under a carport. It appeared that a restoration had been started, then stopped, possibly due to the loss of a job, a baby being born, or simply a lack of interest. Anyway, I knocked on the door, and nobody was home, so we'll never know. Nice car, though.

Driving the Woody east across a quaint bridge on a beautiful autumn day was one of many pleasures of the Barn Find Road Trip.

HOWELL'S AUTO SALES

Car Count	For Sale?
7	YES NO MAYBE

It was Saturday afternoon, and most businesses were closed for the weekend. So, wouldn't you know, we stumbled across a small used car lot and repair shop that had a number of interesting cars scattered about.

And, of course, they were closed.

We were driving down the road and a 1948 or '49 Ford tow truck that was parked perpendicular to the road attracted our attention. Wait, behind the building was a chopped-top 1951 Ford pickup truck. By the time we turned into the lot we saw a 1957 Buick Special, 1946 Hudson, an early Ford cab-over truck, and a nice Datsun 510 (I have a sweet spot in my heart for Datsun 510s, BTW). And inside the building was another old car of unknown origin. We tramped around for 30 minutes or so, looking at the vehicles, and Michael shot some photos, then we were back on the road.

The original Howell's Auto Sales tow truck that Bo Howell's father built decades earlier. Bo found the truck in a scrap yard and bought it as "yard art."

After our trip, I called Howell's and spoke to Bo Howell.

"My father got his dealer's license in 1966, and we've been here ever since," said Bo. "My father built that tow truck in the 1960s and sold it in the '70s or '80s. I found it in a salvage yard

A 1947 Ford pickup sitting at the closed Howell's Auto Sales used car lot. The dealership had a number of special-interest cars that were for sale.

This 1946 Hudson sedan is powered by a Chevy engine and is used by Bo Howell to run errands around town.

and bought it back to use as yard art, because my dad built it. It's not for sale."

But most of the other old cars on his lot were, in fact, for sale.

"The 1957 Buick did run when we first got it, but it needs a total restoration," he said. "I'm asking $1,000 for it. It has a Nailhead V-8 engine.

"The 1951 chopped Ford truck was built by a guy who now works for Richard Childress Racing down in the Carolinas, so I know the work was done well. It has a Camaro subframe installed with a small-block Chevy and a Turbo transmission. It still needs some glass and wiring work, and it needs an interior. I'm asking $7,500 for that truck, but I'm a little flexible."

This slammed '51 Ford pickup has a late-model drivetrain and was built by a NASCAR fabricator. All the heavy work has been performed, and a hobbyist could easily complete the project.

The old car we saw in the garage was a 1935 Studebaker sedan, which had been Frankensteined with a Mustang II front suspension and late model rear.

Sitting near the entrance to Howell's is this 1957 Buick Special. The car is complete, though rough, and can be purchased for $1,000.

Bo explained that the Hudson sedan was a 1946. It also has a small-block Chevy engine with a two-speed Powerglide transmission. It ran well, and he used to drive it to the post office and to pick up parts.

Inside the building, the other car we couldn't identify was a 1935 Studebaker four-door, possibly a Commander model. It has no drivetrain, but is otherwise complete. Someone had started to hot rod the car with a Mustang II front suspension and GM rear.

"There is still an enormous amount of old cars out there," Bo said when I told him of our quest.

Unfortunately, the Datsun 510, a 1971 one-owner car that Bo had tried to buy for 30 years before securing it the past spring, is not for sale. He said he used to race Datsun 510s up and down the East Coast, and he knows them inside and out. This one was a keeper.

The day was beginning to look up!

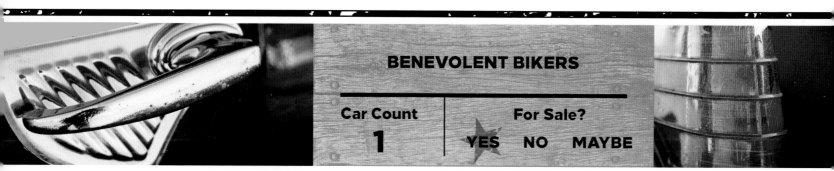

BENEVOLENT BIKERS

Car Count	For Sale?
1	YES NO MAYBE

After leaving Howell's, we drove a little further down the road toward Woolwine, Virginia, and parked the Woody next to a bunch of motorcycle riders who were making a pit stop during their ride on that beautiful Saturday afternoon. In the parking lot next door was a cute little 1949 Plymouth coupe with a For Sale sign on it. So, while Brian and Michael chatted with the bikers, I checked out the coupe.

It was a solid car, either original or an older restoration. It was parked in front of an antique shop, which was closed for the day, so we couldn't discuss the car with anyone. There was a gentleman in the parking lot, however, who said he lived upstairs from the antique store.

This 1949 Plymouth sat outside of an antique store near Woolwine, Virginia, with a For Sale sign in the window. The best thing about stopping here was that a parking lot full of motorcyclists told us about a field of rusty Chevys nearby.

"The owners of that coupe are my landlords," he said. "They have a few other cars as well, including a 1966 Hemi Charger, I think."

As we were saying our goodbyes to the bikers and began to leave, one of them mentioned, "We just passed a whole bunch of rusty old cars from the 1930s and '40s up the road in a guy's yard. Just go straight up this road about 10 miles toward Stuart, and you'll see them."

Well, this was a lead too tempting to pass up, so we continued up the old Woolwine Highway until we saw the rusty cars.

RARE CHEVY BONEYARD

Car Count	For Sale?
11	**YES NO MAYBE**

The first thing I noticed was that the cars were not actually from the 1930s and '40s, as we had been told, but were all Chevys from the 1950s and '60s. And they were rusty, but very cool.

After making a U-turn up the road and doubling back to the yard, we drove up the driveway near the row of rusty Chevys. There was a man using a weed-eater and a woman riding a lawn tractor. I figured they were the homeowners, so we sat in the car and waited for them to acknowledge us. And waited. They either didn't care to talk with us, or they already knew we were going to inquire about the old cars and decided to finish their yard work first.

Finally the man stopped and gave us permission to look at his cars. I asked if I could drive my Woody over for photography purposes, and he said yes, but that we should watch out for snakes. Then he resumed his yard work.

Yikes! Snakes. This car hunting could be hazardous.

This 1957 Chevy sedan delivery has certainly seen better days. This one is certainly a rare body style, though, and could be refurbished by a talented restorer.

The field of purported "1930s and 1940s" Chevys were actually 20 years newer than that. I parked the Woody in the middle of the cars, but worried when the owner told me to watch for the snakes…

Mr. Chevrolet

Wow, here was a row of 11 old Chevys, and not just any old Chevys, but unique body styles. I'll start from the oldest to the newest:

1956 Chevy four-door	1960 Chevy sedan delivery
1956 Chevy sedan delivery	1960 Chevy El Camino
1957 Chevy four-door	1961 Chevy station wagon (four dr.)
1957 Chevy station wagon (two dr.)	1962 Chevy two-door sedan
1957 Chevy sedan delivery	1966 Chevy BelAir (two dr.)
	1967 Chevy Nova

When the man finished mowing, he came over and introduced himself as Gary Vaughn. He is a longtime collector, restorer, and hot rodder of Chevys.

"I sold a bunch of them here lately," said the 64-year-old. "Once I had them all the way across the field. I sold four to a man who came out of Jacksonville, Florida, recently. I sold him three 1956 Chevy Nomads, and he also bought a '56 four-door, because it still had the original drivetrain. And I sold four more to a boy down in Danville [Virginia], a '55 delivery, two '55 210 two-door wagons, and a 210 car.

Another sedan delivery, this one a 1960. Owner Gary Vaughn said he would like to restore it if he can finish his other projects.

"I've been collecting these things forever.

"These cars are for sale. About the only one I might keep is the 1960 sedan delivery. If I live long enough to finish my projects in the garage, I might just get on that delivery. It's the rarest car down there. Chevy only made 2,108 of those, and 800 of those went to Canada."

Gary had worked at a Chevy dealership for more than 30 years, starting after he got out of the service, so he does all the mechanical work himself.

"I worked in my garage every night. I've always fooled with Chevrolets."

He explained that he has been dragging cars home since the 1970s from all over the South.

"That '61 down there still has the 348-cubic-inch installed," he said. "And the '62, the reason I bought it is because it has a 327/300 horsepower, three-speed with overdrive, and a Posi rear."

Inside Gary's garage, he showed us a couple of the cars he was currently restoring, a 1966 Chevelle SS with a small-block 300-horsepower engine. He also has a 1957 Chevy into which he recently installed front disc brakes.

"I was fixing a Nomad for my son, but he didn't like it because he said it was a family car," he said.

I asked Gary if there was any particular car he was searching for. "The only car I'd like to find is a nice 1960 El Camino. I've had a bunch of '60s over the years."

Gary said that since he worked for Chevrolet for so many years, not only had he learned how to work on the cars, but he also squirreled away lots of N.O.S. parts over the years.

"I have two or three factory tri-power setups for 348 engines. Finding 409 stuff is just about impossible. You just don't find 409 stuff. And I've got couple of brand-new

This 1960 Chevy El Camino is in restorable condition. Gary has many of the parts to restore these cars, including N.O.S. trim and body parts.

aluminum two-four-barrel intake manifolds for 1956 Chevys with the batwing air cleaner and the dual-point distributors. These were optional on Corvettes and passenger cars. 1956 was a year by itself, and the 1957 through '61 had a different casting number.

"I used to go to Charlotte AutoFair for 30-something years and bought up all the N.O.S. stuff, and now I've got buildings full of fenders and hoods from the early 1950s to 1972."

He took us for a tour of his outbuildings, which included brand-new chrome trim, Wonderbar radios, and multiple sets of Chevelle fenders, pickup parts, and rocker panels.

"I bought all these at dealerships," he said. "They used to send out inventory reports with outdated parts that dealers had in stock. If they had a bunch of stuff, I'd just load up and go. Once in the 1970s, I went up to Winchester, Virginia, and came home with all the old parts I could haul."

Gary explained that the economy in the Stuart, Virginia, area was extremely depressed. At one time, textile and furniture manufacturing were the major area industries, but those businesses were now closed.

We said goodbye to Gary and hit the road toward Stuart.

— ON THE ROAD —

It was 6:04 p.m. and the sun was beginning to set, so we decided it was a good time to begin heading to our hotel, which was in Lynchburg, about two hours away. But before we had gone too many miles, we slammed on the brakes and once again made a U-turn at a sight that was too good to believe.

On both sides of the road, and well back into the woods, sat dozens and dozens of old cars from the 1930s to the 1970s. This was the kind of scene that dreams are made of! We had thought the day's mother lode was the recent discovery of Gary Vaughn's old Chevys, but this discovery had that one beat by a mile!

Minutes down the road, we stumbled across Clyde Turner's Used Cars. The former junkyard once contained 1,000 cars. Only about 100 remain.

MEET CLYDE TURNER

Car Count	For Sale?
100	YES NO MAYBE

Within the next two hours we would just scratch the surface of knowing Clyde Turner, who is part junkyard owner, politician, storyteller, faith healer, and salesman. And he's a bit of a country music singer as well. (He talked me into buying his newly released CD…) In other words, Clyde is the ideal southerner. And one of the most interesting people I'd ever met.

Clyde lives among a hundred old cars. Thankfully, most are parked in huge sheds he has constructed around his property to keep them out of the elements. I parked my Woody in his driveway, and before I could even knock on the door, Clyde was already walking toward us with a big smile on his face.

"Glad to meet you, fellows," he said. "Nice car you have there."

"We were driving down the road looking for old cars and saw yours," I said. "How many cars do you have?"

"Well, I used to have 1,000, but I only have about 100 now," he said as we sat down and chatted about his cars and his life.

I asked Clyde if he had any favorite cars.

"That 1940 Ford coupe was my first car," he said. "I bought it for $375 when I was 17 years old. It was the first car I ever drove. I went on my first date in that car, I got my first kiss in that car, my first piece of ass in that car, and I married that woman. She's in the house cooking dinner right now."

(above) Part country music performer, part snake-oil salesman, part storyteller and used car salesman, here's Clyde Turner "hisself."

(below) A particularly clean Falcon Futura sits protected from the weather under a roof. Virtually every car Clyde owns is for sale.

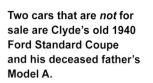

Clyde told me his father was a local entrepreneur: he operated a liquor still, ran moonshine, and farmed.

At one time, cars littered much of his 100-acre property. But as the price of scrap metal rose over the past couple of decades, Clyde started to have his cars crushed. Most of the cars that remain are either pretty solid drivers or restoration candidates. Today, Clyde would not be so quick to crush cars. "People who crush cars will live to regret it in a few months or years," he said. "That's because all the steel goes to China."

These days he sells and rents out his vintage cars for various events. "I rent cars out for movies and TV shows," he said.

Once Sally Fields dropped by to give Clyde an autographed picture because of the cars he had provided for one of her movies. He displays that photo and hundreds of others in his country store, where he sits all day and holds court, tap dances, does magic acts, caters to his pig and rooster, and watches his dog perform tricks for visitors.

Just about every car that Clyde owns is for sale, except for the 1940 Ford coupe and the Model A Ford his father drove. But don't expect to pull a fast one on old Clyde; there are no deals. He knows the value of his cars and gives nothing away.

Clyde Turner is nobody's fool.

Two cars that are *not* for sale are Clyde's old 1940 Ford Standard Coupe and his deceased father's Model A.

This 1949 Ford might be better served as a parts car rather than a restoration candidate. The cars stored under roofs are in much better condition.

—— TIRED BUT HAPPY ——

The visit to Clyde Turner's left us exhausted. Never in a million years did we imagine that, on a day when we hadn't discovered our first interesting old car until early afternoon, by sunset we would stumble into the incredible find we found in Stuart that evening.

Rather than continue more than two hours to Lynchburg, Virginia, to a Hampton Inn where we had already phoned in reservations earlier, we decided to look for a hotel in nearby Martinsville. The road to Lynchburg was rural, and the headlights on the Woody were not the best. We felt that the potential to hit a deer was too great.

Our decision to find a closer hotel room turned out to be quite fortuitous, as it would open up a huge discovery for us the very next morning.

Sheds throughout the property have kept many of Clyde's cars in pretty good condition.

— HOT TIP AT MOUNTAIN JAX —

After we dropped our luggage off at the hotel, we asked the front desk clerk if there were any local pubs in the area. All three of us preferred locally owned restaurants in downtown settings rather than franchise restaurants near highways or shopping malls.

We were advised to go to Mountain Jax in downtown Martinsville, just a couple of miles away. We found it easily and parked the Woody on Main Street in a prime spot in front of the pub. No sooner had we turned off the ignition than the car started to attract attention.

The Woody was doing its job as our calling card.

Our plan was to mine for leads each night in local pubs, but I was not at all optimistic about scoring a find for the next day. Many southern families go to church on Sunday mornings, then usually go out to lunch. So I didn't expect to do much more than drive around until early- to mid-afternoon.

Boy was I wrong!

As we entered the pub, sat down, and ordered a burger and a beer, people started to ask us about our Woody and what were we doing on a Saturday night

Our bartender at Mountain Jax, Molly Hatchet, became a good friend and valuable guide.

in Martinsville. When we told them we were writing a book about looking for old cars, we became the most exciting guys in town!

Our bartender that evening was named Molly Hatchet. We had to ask about her name.

"My parents liked the band so much back in the '70s that they decided to name me after them," she said.

Molly was a sweet local girl who acted as our goodwill ambassador, introducing us to locals who might know of some old car collections. Within a couple of hours, we cracked the code about how to find interesting old cars on a Sunday morning in the South. I met a gentleman,

Danny Turner, who, after learning of our mission, took out his cell phone and called his friend, A. C. Wilson.

"I'll bet A. C. would love to meet you guys in the morning," said Danny.

I spoke to A. C. for a few minutes on the phone, and we agreed to meet at his property at 7:30 a.m. Sunday morning, which was just nine hours from then.

He promised to show us enough cars to keep us happy, although he could only spend about one-and-a-half hours with us because he had to drive to Roanoke to attend church.

We said good night to Molly and the rest of the Mountain Jax patrons and staff, and high-tailed it back to our hotel; tomorrow would come way too quickly.

DAY

3

We woke up early, grabbed our free breakfast in the dining room just off the lobby, and started to head for the door when we were stopped by the desk clerk. He said that the kind lady who had checked us in the evening before was intrigued with our car-hunting story and had left information for us about a restored older gas station nearby. She thought that we might like to park our Woody next to the station for photos.

We didn't want to be late for our appointment with A. C., so we took the information, thanked the clerk and headed out the door.

We thought that if we had time later, we would check out the restored gas station. We never actually made it there, but appreciate the hotel clerk's kind gesture. It shows that Southern Hospitality is alive and well!

There isn't much wood left on this Buick Woody. This relic has certainly seen its last surfin' safari…

(top) Who could imagine that early on a Sunday morning we would be standing in front of a collection of cars like this? Despite the rust, it was a sight for sore eyes.

(left) A late model Cadillac sits in a sea of Buicks, Lincolns, older Caddys, and a lone sedan delivery.

**BUICKS AND CADDYS
ON SUNDAY MORNING**

Car Count	For Sale?		
75	YES	NO	MAYBE

We drove to the address A. C. had given us on the phone the night before, and met him just as he was getting out of his car.

A. C. was a refined southern gentleman, who would likely look more comfortable in a business suit than under a greasy old car, but greasy cars were his thing, and he was about to share his passion with us.

The cars were located adjacent to an RV park he owned on Tensbury Drive in Martinsville. He told us that Tensbury Drive was once a major north-south travel route that went from Maine to Florida prior to the interstate highway boom. Brian confirmed this by telling us that in fact his grandparents drove his mother in their 1949 Ford down this very road from Buffalo, New York, to Key West, Florida, in 1955.

This garaged 1952 Buick Roadmaster has only 16,000 miles on the odometer. The body is rust-free, and the original paint could probably be buffed out.

"They dropped off my mom at the navy base where my dad was stationed in Key West," he said. "They drove down my Dad's Ford, which was his hot rod."

Tensbury Drive had been alternately known as both Old Route 220 and Highway 31. It was hard to believe that Brian's mom and grandparents drove right past this location some 60 years earlier. As we were walking back to see the cars behind the fence, Danny Turner—the gentleman who had told us about A. C. the night before at Mountain Jax pub—drove up.

A. C. had about 75 cars, mostly Buicks and Cadillacs, that he had been buying since his teens. A. C. did what we all should have done; bought cars when they were cheap and held onto them. Unfortunately, most of the cars had been sitting outside for decades, so, at least to me, they appeared to be mostly parts cars.

"I've lived in Martinsville my whole life," he said. "My father used to say, 'Son, you can look, but you can't buy, because we just don't have the money.' But my uncle was a Buick dealer in [nearby] Radford. So I used to go to his dealership, and he'd let me sit in the cars, which was a good way to get infected with the car disease.

VINTAGE GAS STATION

W e never made it to the vintage gas station, but wanted to provide information for readers who might find themselves in the area.

It's a vintage Shell station, and the address is Fieldale Antiques, 478 Field Ave, Fieldale, Virginia. The phone number is 276-336-2536.

The website Roadside America says, "It's worth a detour."

The interior of this '52 Roadmaster is like new. With minimal work, this car could be entered in the Preservation class at a Concours d'Elegance.

A. C. Wilson, the man who assembled a field full of mostly Buicks and Cadillacs, was getting ready to leave for church after he said goodbye to us that Sunday morning.

"So eventually we had a little rock quarry, so I'd buy old cars and store them up there out of sight so my dad didn't see them. Nobody gave me grief about them. But years later when I sold the quarry, I had to move them down here."

As I walked around the rows of cars, I saw numbers written on them in crayon.

"What do those numbers mean," I asked A. C.

"My brother gives me grief about keeping all these old cars, so I've decided to auction them all," he said. An auction was held two months after we visited.

A. C. said that even though most of the cars he owns were acquired locally, occasionally he'd travel to places like Pennsylvania to buy a car with attractive options, like factory air conditioning, to use on another project.

Since selling the quarry, A. C. told me his main businesses are real estate and the R.V. park, which was just 100 yards from where we were standing. And he was also in the process of restoring two old houses on the New River.

I asked A. C. which cars he saw as the best restoration candidates. "Well, there's the 1955 Buick that could use a good paint job that would be nearly ready to go," he said. "I bought it because it had no rust.

"And there's that 1956 Buick that has factory air conditioning on it."

A. C. explained that his father finally got used to the idea of his son buying old cars.

"I once purchased a '66 Lincoln Continental and brought my father with me on a trip in it to Richmond, and it had such a wonderful ride that

This 1939 Buick convertible was enough to make a lifetime Ford man weak in the knees. The car survived the Pearl Harbor bombings.

A. C. Wilson inherited this car from his aunt with only 23,000 miles on the odometer. He drove it to college for four years,0 and the car now has 65,000 miles on it.

he got quite happy in this old car business. This change happened over the course of just one weekend," he said.

A. C. was a Buick man, though, through and through.

"Not only because my uncle owned the dealership, but my grandmother bought a new Buick in 1940 when she was 80 years old, and we still own that car today," he said.

We were invited to look at the cars he kept in his garage. One look, and we instantly saw that A. C. didn't just own rusty parts cars, but fine restored and original examples as well.

One car that got our attention was a 1952 Buick Roadmaster with just 16,000 miles on it. He discovered it years ago when he was driving his 1952 Buick station wagon and stopped at a garage to get a quart of oil. When the mechanic lifted the garage door, it revealed the sedan. The interior on this 62-year-old car still looked new. It featured power seats, Dynaflow transmission, and a Nailhead V-8 producing 180 horsepower.

An odd juxtaposition. We visited friends at Virginia International Raceway and parked the Woody in the SASCO paddock next to a Lola T-70.

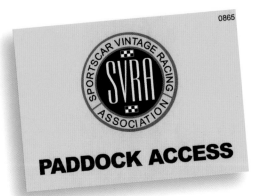

"This Cadillac over there was purchased new by my mother's sister, and it was left to me in her will," said A. C. "I got it when it had 23,000 miles on it. I was a student back then, and I was the only student to arrive in a Cadillac to college. My father, who was a farm guy, was quite embarrassed by it." Despite driving it to college for four years, it still had only 65,000 miles on the odometer.

I asked him if any of his cars had interesting histories. He then led us to another room in his garage.

"Well, I have this 1939 Buick that my aunt owned in Hawaii, where it was sitting on the dock when the Japanese bombed Pearl Harbor," he said.

Indeed he did have cars with interesting histories. The Buick before me was enough to make this longtime Ford man weak in the knees.

"My mother's sister married a guy in the Naval Academy," he said. "When he graduated they moved to Hawaii where he was assigned to the USS PENSACOLA, which sailed out of Hawaii."

Departing from VIR, we headed north through the rural tobacco fields of Virginia.

"While he was out on maneuvers for six days, the bombing happened. This car sat on Dock C, and did not get damaged. So when he steamed back into port, he knew the country was at war. It was a scary time, and nobody knew if Hawaii was going to be bombed again.

"So the original owner of this Buick gave the title, the keys, and the car to my mother's sister's husband. My aunt stayed in Hawaii for a year and worked in a Quonset hut, where she monitored war-time radio transmissions, thinking that the Japanese were going to come back any day."

Her husband was thought to be dead, captured by the Japanese while on maneuvers. But he was in fact a P.O.W. in the South Pacific.

"After a year, she and the Buick boarded a ship destined for San Francisco. When she reached the California port, she drove the car to Radford, Virginia, which took 14 or 15 days.

"They had many, many [tire] blowouts, which was why it took so long."

One night, right after the war was finally over, A. C.'s aunt, who thought her husband was dead, received a phone call from a man in Seattle, Washington. He said he had just received a short-wave-radio message from her husband, who was alive and had asked his wife to wait for him.

Her husband finally arrived home and ended up at Walter Reed Hospital for rehabilitation after the war was over.

"Eventually he was promoted to rear admiral. He and my aunt had four children, and they moved all around the country," said A. C. "They used this car for all their moves; it led an interesting life. This is the third engine, and it probably has 300,000 miles on it."

A. C. told us that eventually the car would not shift into gear—something had come apart in the shift mechanism—so it was parked in his aunt's garage for years. A. C. would ask his aunt from time to time if he could have the car, but the answer was always no, that she would offer it to her own two sons. But her sons were more interested in airplanes than cars, so A. C. was finally given the car around 1974.

A. C. kept the car stored in a shed for 20 years before a woman he was dating said that he needed to get that car running again. So he sent it off to Lewis Jenkins—a Buick specialist—in North Wilkesboro, North Carolina, to have restored.

He told us that even this prized 1939 Buick was going to be sold at auction. Totaling more than 75, A. C. was going to auction off all his cars.

HOLY HAY CASTLE!

Driving through the country on the way to Lynchburg, Virginia, we passed something I had never seen before—a hay castle.

Maybe I'm just a city slicker, but this was an entirely new concept to all three of us. We had to explore it. It was castle-like in size and shape, but was made entirely of bales of hay. People pay money to climb up it and crawl through it. For a kid, this would be a fantasy!

I spoke with some of the employees, and the owner—A. J. Nuckols—about the project.

Nuckols owns the 20-acre White Hall Farm, which had been a tobacco farm but for the last 20 years, has mostly grown pumpkins. He came up with the concept of building a castle from hay about 6 years ago, and it's been a popular seasonal attraction for residents ever since.

He said that charging admission to folks to explore the hay castle is just a way for a farmer to supplement his family's income. And from the size of the crowd waiting to get in, it looked like business was brisk.

Interestingly, whereas the Woody had been a most popular vehicle wherever we drove, Nuckols and the rest of the staff were more interested in the Ford Flex! They were looking that vehicle over with a find-tooth comb. Being farmers, they saw the practicality of the Flex being more useful than the Woody.

To get a better idea of what a hay castle is, go to www.whitefallfarm.com.

"I want to get down to zero," he said.

Brian asked about the black 1966 Lincoln Continental sedan that was also destined for the auction block. It was the very Lincoln that had convinced A. C.'s father that vintage cars were OK.

"That's a Martinsville car since new," said A. C. about the Lincoln. "It was bought new by the owner of a dairy. Then the Piedmont Bank president bought it and called me one day and told me he was going to sell it.

"'Bring me $400 and it's yours,' he said. I drove it for 10 years and never did anything mechanical to it. It's really classy."

Brian confided that his own father had always dreamed of owning a black Lincoln like that one. He immediately started scheming on how he could buy that car from A. C. before it reached the auction block…

Our morning was well spent with A. C., but he reminded us he needed to start heading toward Roanoke for church.

Welcome to the annual Hay Castle at Nuckol's Farm. Folks pay to climb on and explore inside this incredible structure.

So we bid farewell and headed down the road. Since our morning was so productive, we felt we could justify a couple of hours at Virginia International Raceway, where a few friends of mine were competing in that weekend's vintage races. Besides, we only needed to be back in Roanoke in the morning, so we had some time to kill. We wanted to investigate British Auto Restorations and King's Restorations near Cloverdale, both of which we had heard about the day before. But until then, we'd enjoy seeing some great cars, friends, and racing. And who knows, we might even get a barn-find lead from someone at the track.

We didn't' actually hear about any barn finds at the track, but we mooched lunch from the great folks at SASCO Sports, who sometimes service my 1964 Corvette road-racing car. Thanks, Dave and Robyn Handy!

Wow, this was an OK day.

That evening we stayed in a Hampton Inn, our lodging of choice, in Lynchburg, Virginia. We would head back to Roanoke first thing in the morning so we could check out some of the leads we had heard about the week prior.

That evening we ate at a really cool pizzeria and microbrewery, Waterstone Pizza and the Jefferson Street Brewery. The pizza pub was housed in a great old building, which was a cornerstone in the city's historic district revitalization.

We had some excellent pizza and sampled some craft brews, and even though we did not hear about any old car finds, had a wonderful evening.

The folks at the farm were much more interested in the 2014 Ford Flex than the Woody. Way to go Ford!

DAY

4

On the way to Roanoke, we went past an interesting trucking company that had a vintage school bus parked perpendicular to the road.

It was a Studebaker, that was unmistakable. I certainly recognized the pleasant lines and smiley grill of a Studebaker pickup truck, but had never seen a Studebaker school bus before. And this was not a standard school bus, but a short bus, one that might have been used in a rural community. And it was for sale. It was pretty cool, and could definitely have been converted into some kind of unusual hot rod camper.

Nobody was home, so I took a good look at the unique vehicle, inside and out.

The first things I noticed were the two pot-metal "Cal Custom" styled scoops that were installed on the hood. This modification was probably done after the bus'

Commonwealth Auto Sales had a number of cars that had potential, including this 1955 Ford two-door sedan with a 1957 312. It runs.

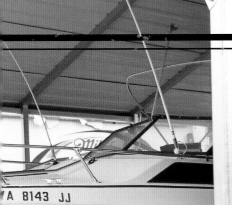

(top) I had never seen a Studebaker school bus before—especially a miniature version—so we had to stop for a closer look. It was a pretty cool vehicle with a lot of potential.

(left) Obviously someone had used this as a camper at one time.

SCHOOL HOUSE ROCK

Car Count	For Sale?
1	**YES NO MAYBE**

kid-hauling days were over. I remember seeing those scoops in J. C. Whitney catalogues in the 1960s.

Inside the bus I noticed another aftermarket modification: a Moon gas pedal; the type that would have been used on a hot rod, or an early Bonneville streamliner. It became apparent that a hot rodder had had some influence on this bus at some time in its life.

I wondered if it had an interesting engine transplant? Maybe a Chrysler Hemi or a big-block Chevy? Nope. When I lifted the hood, a flathead six-cylinder sat obediently in the engine bay.

Since nobody was around, I called the phone number on the For Sale sign. I had a wonderful conversation with Bonnie Reed, who, along with her husband, bought it a couple of years earlier but never got around to restoring it.

So they were selling it.

SBD—these cars have seen better days. This 1963 Thunderbird (one of two) and 1953 Chevy sedan are pretty rough, but are for sale for either parts or restoration.

Bonnie told me the short bus was called a two-and-a-half window and was fabricated by the Wayne Body Company. The price was $8,500. I thanked her and told her I would keep it in mind if I met anyone looking for a school bus project.

Within a few miles of the school bus, we saw a rather disheveled, yet interesting, yard full of old cars. There were some familiar roundish shapes of 1950s vehicles, as well as those with more angular 1960s designs.

(clockwise from left) This 1957 Ford is for sale but without an engine. The original powerplant went into the 1955 Ford.

As soon as the owner can iron out the title for this Studebaker Silver Hawk, it will also be for sale.

The car that got us most excited was this 1963 Rambler 202. It was purchased soon after we saw it, and will appear in a feature-length movie that was filmed nearby.

HONEST JACK'S
USED CARS

Car Count	For Sale?		
10	YES	NO	MAYBE

We pulled the Woody and the Flex into the parking lot and walked toward the adjacent commercial building. It was called Commonwealth Auto Sales and was run by Jack Smith. Jack told me we were free to roam the premises and take all the photos we wanted.

"I've run this place for 30 years," Jack said. I suppose at one time, this was a thriving business on the main road, but over the ensuing 30 years his used cars just sat for a long time. Eventually the grasses and bushes grew up into trees, engulfing the cars. Clearly this business had seen better days. The roof in the service area had collapsed in a recent windstorm, so Jack worked in a shop with a 20-foot sunroof over his head. Sad.

Brian, Michael, and I made our way around the yard, and amid dozens and dozens of old cars, we did notice a few "gems" that could be restored. These included:

1953 Chevy two-door	1962 Ford T-Bird
1955 Ford two-door	1963 Rambler 202 two-door
1955 Ford four-door	1963 T-Bird
1957 Ford Fairlane	1963 Pontiac Grand Prix
1957 Studebaker Silver Hawk	1964 Chevy Impala

Additionally there were a couple of older trucks—early 1950s Chevy pickups—that were too far-gone for restoration but had parts potential. The car I was most attracted to, surprisingly, was the little 1963 Rambler 202 two-door back in the rear corner. I asked Jack about the car.

"I bought it about two or three years ago," he said. "When I got it, the gas tank was all corroded, and it needed a rebuilt carburetor and fuel pump."

When I asked him how much that car would sell for, he said he'd like to keep it from the crusher.

"I have about $1,500 invested in it," he said. "I'd take that much for it."

Jack Smith has owned Commonwealth for decades and knows his way around older cars. All his cars are for sale, as well as maybe some of the Camaros he has at his house.

Wow, that was a pretty good-looking car, and the price was very fair. If I hadn't sworn off any new automotive purchases, I would have actually considered it myself.

"I buy most of my cars to keep them from going to the junkyards," he said.

I asked Jack about another decent car, the 1955 Ford two-door.

"That belongs to a friend of mine. I was supposed to restore it for him, but he's got a heart problem, so now he wants me to sell it for him. He wants $5,500 for it. He also owns the 1957 Ford next to it. When he got them, they were both running, driving cars. But his son-in-law pulled the engines out of both cars, then put the 312 engine out of the '57 into the '55 instead of the 272.

"So my friend got mad and put both cars in the garage for years. Then he brought both cars over here to have me get them running. The '55 has a three-speed on the column with a new clutch disc, pressure plate, and throw-out bearing in it. It runs real good. He was deciding what to do with the 272 engine, and then he got heart problems, so he decided to sell them both."

Jack's friend is asking $3,500 for the nonrunning 1957 Ford.

The 1957 Studebaker Silver Hawk belongs to the same friend. "Until he gets the title straightened out on that car, he doesn't want to sell that one," he said.

I asked Jack if he had any old cars himself.

"Yeah, I have a 1963 Pontiac Grand Prix, a '64 Impala, and I've got a bunch of '68, '69, and '70 Camaros at home."

We took our photos, said goodbye to Jack, and continued on our path back toward Roanoke, a city that we believed still hid many automotive treasures.

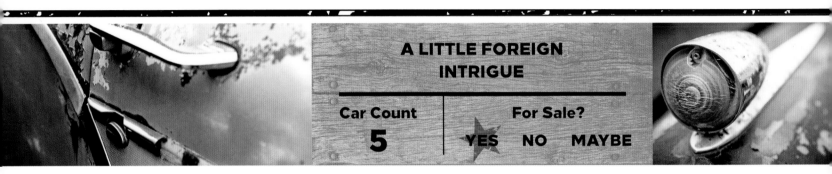

A LITTLE FOREIGN INTRIGUE

Car Count	For Sale?		
5	YES	NO	MAYBE

We had heard about British Auto Restorations in Roanoke from a couple of people at the Saturday cruise-in. But we had to wait until Monday to investigate because they were closed on weekends.

When we arrived at their shop, I noticed cleanliness, not a back lot filled with old sports cars in various stages of deterioration. One of the things I especially enjoy about visiting traditional sports car shops is the pile of crap lying around in the back.

There was no crap that I could see, just a tidy parking lot and a respectable building. Hmmm. Maybe the business was closed?

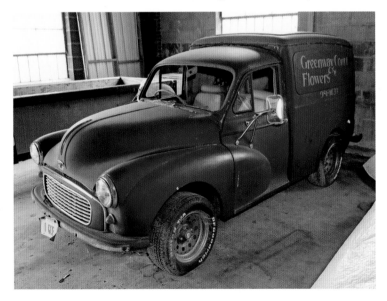

This cool Morris Minor panel van at British Auto Restorations is probably not for sale, but it has been sitting in storage for many years.

I walked in the front door and quickly discovered that they were very much in business. There were several British sports cars undergoing ground-up restorations, as well as a couple of customer cars in for service.

I introduced myself to one of the business's two owners, Tyson Smith. He and his brother, Ted, are partners; they started the business 20 years ago and have developed a reputation for performing quality work.

But where were all the old cars? I was soon to find out. Tyson had a small warehouse just up the street where he kept cars out of the weather.

"These are mostly customer cars," said Tyson as we walked into the storage building. "We store customer cars here during the winter time, or while we're waiting for parts."

We walked inside the building, and once our eyes adjusted to the darkness, we were impressed with the all cars that surrounded us. There was a terrific little Morris Minor delivery van that had been used by a local flower shop, a very proper Jaguar E-Type, an Austin Healey 3000, a Rolls Royce, Mercedes 450 SLC, Triumph TR250, etc.

Tyson revealed that his own personal passion was for Triumph TR3s.

"I sold the last nice one I had a couple of years ago," he said. "But these days I have lots of sports cars that need to be driven. They are my customers' cars, and they all need to be exercised.

"My brother and I loved these old British sports cars when we were kids, drove them hard and lived to tell about it," he said. "Our dad had a dealership up in Parkersburg, West Virginia, that sold MGs. And we had an old Arnolt MGTD with Bertone bodywork. We passed that thing back and forth between each other for a while, then we got into the Triumphs. I wish we would have kept that old MG, though."

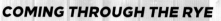

COMING THROUGH THE RYE

Friend Zach Straits had been following the progress of our road trip on social media. We met Zach for dinner one night, and, when he asked what interesting cars we had discovered so far, I mentioned the cute Rambler 202.

"There's a movie being shot in [nearby] Orange, Virginia, [called] *Coming Through the Rye*, and I think they are looking for a 1963 Rambler." Well, Zach mentioned the Rambler to one of the folks involved in securing cars for the movie, and they wound up buying the car. But first they had Jack at Commonwealth Auto Sales perform some mechanical work to make it reliable. For instance, because the gas tank was rusted, a racing-type fuel cell was installed. You can read about the movie at www.comingthroughtheryemovie.com.

When I saw Zach at the Muscle Car and Corvette Nationals in Chicago two months later, I asked him how the little Rambler was performing since going from the junkyard to its new Hollywood career.

"It's running well, but when I sat inside it, my feet went through the floor."

I'm sure that scene will be cut from the movie.

Although these Triumph TR3s are rough, there are enough of them that at least one complete car could be fabricated. Additionally, the owners of British Auto Restorations have loads of spare parts for Triumphs.

Both brothers worked for the Norfolk Southern railroad before retiring and hanging out their own shingle as restorers. "We wanted to do something we liked to do before we died, which was restoring British cars, so now it's been 20 years full-time."

Tyson said the thing he enjoys most are his clients, many of whom have become personal friends. Their shop just completed restoring a 1947 Rolls Royce for one customer. It took five years.

"We've done a bunch of cars over the years."

He said they prefer restoring cars to "driver" condition instead of show cars, because restoring to the higher level is so much more costly and time-consuming.

The cars that are for sale are Tyson's Triumph TR3s. In all honesty, the Triumphs are in pretty rough condition, but he had several of them. And Tyson certainly had enough spare Triumph parts to restore almost anything; the roof over the office in his garage was lined with dozens of TR3 doors, hoods, and fenders.

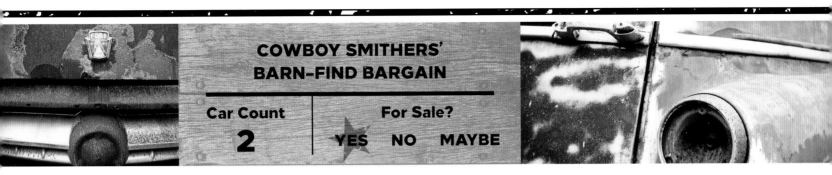

COWBOY SMITHERS' BARN-FIND BARGAIN

Car Count	For Sale?
2	YES NO MAYBE

We said goodbye to Tyson but didn't go far. Sitting in a vacant lot next to his storage building were two interesting basket cases: a 1954 Ford Courier, which is a sedan delivery; and a 1950-something Studebaker Silver Hawk. It seems as though old cars attract more old cars. I suppose looser zoning regulations in industrial areas, in addition to lower rental rates, make those areas more attractive for old car hobbyists.

We contacted the cars' owner, Billy "Cowboy" Smithers, who is no stranger to searching for old cars. He said he knew of a field with more than 200 cars parked there, including a 1969 440 Charger with a four-speed, a 1969 Camaro SS, a Cobra Jet Ford Mustang, and more.

"I'd take $2,500 for the two cars (the '54 Ford and the Studebaker)," Billy said. They were not in great shape, but the price was certainly fair for street rod material.

(above) Directly next to British Auto Restorations' storage facility sat a couple of other relics that were for sale, like this Ford Courier and a bright green Studebaker Silver Hawk.

(left) Ford Couriers are rare vehicles. Though this 1954 model has seen better days, the car still has much potential and is for sale.

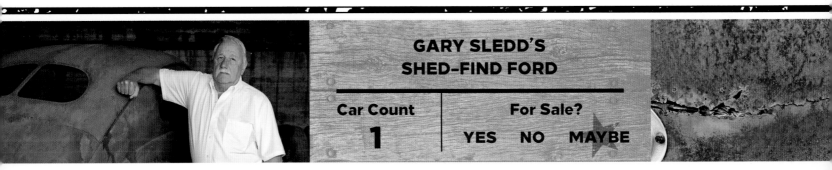

GARY SLEDD'S
SHED-FIND FORD

Car Count	For Sale?
1	YES NO MAYBE

Tyson from British Auto Restorations told us the building next door to his had a number of American muscle cars and hot rods inside. Tyson gave us the building owner's phone number, and we were soon met by Gary Sledd.

Gary was a successful businessman who is now semi-retired, which means he has time to spend messing around with his old cars. He invited us inside and showed us his collection, which included two beautiful 1957 Chevys, a Nova, a Fairlane GT, 1956 Ford Crown Victoria, and a Mustang GT. And he owned a freshly built, hot rodded 1940 Ford coupe.

We liked Gary's cars, but we told him we were not here to see his beautiful cars, but instead to photograph and discuss ugly barn finds. Did he have any?

Old cars seem to gather in the same neighborhood. This 1940 Ford Standard sedan is in a building next to the cars in the previous four photos. It's got a honking 318 Chrysler installed, and might be available.

As a matter of fact, he had just recently removed a rather rough 1940 Ford two-door sedan from a barn just 1 mile from where we were standing. It was a rather odd combination of parts: the nose was from a 1940 Ford Deluxe, and the main body was from a 1940 Ford Standard, complete with one taillight. Someone had installed a Chrysler 318-cubic-inch engine and a Torqueflite automatic transmission with a Ford 9-inch rear axle.

"They said it was running recently," said Gary. "Someone

was making a hot rod out of it. The frame was solid, and they didn't want much money for it. I don't know if I'll fix it up or sell it. I know from restoring the coupe that these front fenders with no rust are worth a fair bit of money."

We said goodbye to Gary and thanked him for his time. It was time to head for another foreign car shop we were told about, Webb Motors, on the other side of town.

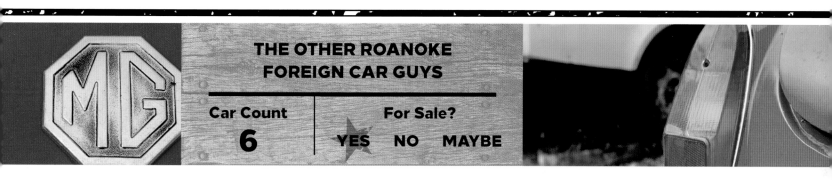

THE OTHER ROANOKE FOREIGN CAR GUYS

Car Count	For Sale?		
6	YES	NO	MAYBE

Back in the heyday of sports and import cars in the United States, Webb Motors was the center of the universe for enthusiasts in the Roanoke area. I walked in and met Mark Hancock. Mark had been associated with Webb Motors as a young guy in 1970 until 1981, when he actually bought the company.

"I eventually left and went into commercial banking but retired from banking about two years ago and came back here to help them out a little bit," he said. "And I never left."

Some of the cars behind Webb Motors include an MGB and a Triumph TR7.

The basement at Webb is where the real treasures are hidden. This almost new, but flood-damaged Simca holds numerous wiring harnesses. New rollbars sit on the floor.

At one time, Webb Motors had been a British Motor Corporation, then British Leyland, dealership, selling MGs, Triumphs, Austin Healeys, and Hillman at this location since 1957. The business is still owned by Byron Webb, the son of the founder. In its prime, Webb Motors was also a motorcycle dealership that sold the Vincent, Indian, and Matchless brands.

Mark showed me some cars around the rear of the building that he said were probably good enough to be restored at one time, but now are better suited as parts cars or race car projects.

There were a couple of MGBs, one of which was made up of two cars, a 1965 front and a 1970 rear. There were also a couple of Midgets that had seen better days.

In the showroom were a number of very nice sports cars, a few original and a few restored, that were being sold by Webb for their owners on consignment.

But the real gold mine here was the huge vintage sports car parts inventory in the basement. Over the decades, enough new and used parts, Lucas and otherwise, accumulated in the basement that could satisfy nearly any British enthusiast. In addition, there was a strange little Simca. Apparently, at one time, Webb had also been a Simca dealer in addition to all the British marques.

"That car was our original Simca demonstrator," said Dexter Bradbury, who has been at Webb for 25 years. "The owner had a green Simca and his brother had the gold one that is now in the basement. That one went through the flood of 1985, so they towed it over here, and it's been sitting the basement ever since."

They mentioned that all the parts cars, in addition to the Simca, would be for sale.

Before we left Webb Motors, they recommended we talk to a man named John Eldridge, who they said owned a barn full of old sports cars. I called John and couldn't believe what I heard. John said he owned more than 100 sports cars, mostly MGs, and that they were stored in several locations in the Roanoke area.

I told John that we were leaving Roanoke in order to stay on our road trip schedule. But we made an appointment to meet when we came back through the Roanoke area after we left Hershey. A visit to John's collection would be an exciting conclusion to our adventure!

HOOK AND LADDER

Car Count	For Sale?
1	YES NO MAYBE

When we left Webb, we drove through an older part of Roanoke and came upon a giant old hook-and-ladder fire truck that was sitting in the corner of a parking lot. We thought it would be cool to include a piece of heavy equipment in this book, so we stopped to take a look.

The fire truck is owned by the Roanoke Firefighters Union, who had an office in the adjacent building, but they didn't know much about it. Luckily Brian had some friends in upstate New York who collect and restore old fire trucks, and he sent them a text. Within minutes it was all over social media and information started arriving on his iPhone. This is what he found out:

The truck is a 1940 American La France with a 100-foot tiller. It was formerly Truck #1, delivered in Battleship Gray to the Roanoke Fire

Brian, our heavy-equipment specialist, had to fulfill a boyhood fantasy about steering the hook-and-ladder from the rear!

And now for something completely different—we stumbled upon this 1940 American La France hook-and-ladder truck sitting in a parking lot.

Department and repainted red in the 1960s. The Seagraves was still in service in 1979, when it was stationed downtown. The roof light is a Federal Beacon Ray, which was introduced in 1948. The wooden ladders are still original to the truck.

It has not been started in at least 15 years. It was purchased by the Roanoke Firefighters Union from the Virginia Transportation Museum with the intention of restoring it. This has not happened due to lack of donations. So it sits.

We were told, though, that perhaps they might consider selling it. Do you still have the childhood dream of becoming a fireman?

— OUR VIRGINIA CONNECTION —

One of the folks who had been following our journey on social media was Zach Strait. For those of you who have read my most recent barn-find book, *50 Shades of Rust*, you may remember the great story of Zach's car, a 1967 Camaro SS/RS that he inherited from his grandmother, who bought it new.

Zach lived in nearby Staunton, Virginia, and sent me a text saying we needed to connect while we were in the area because he knew of a couple of interesting cars he

The street-level showroom at Bruce Elder's Staunton, Virginia, dealership features about 50 special-interest cars that are for sale, including this Continental Mk II.

wanted us to see. He told us an interesting story about a 429 Torino that had been sitting in one spot for decades. That certainly got my interest.

He said we could visit that car the next morning. But tonight he arranged for us to visit his friend Bruce Elder, who operates a special-interest car dealership out of an old Staunton, Virginia, Ford dealership that had been built in 1911.

Great! Sign us up!

LIVING THE DREAM, LITERALLY

Car Count	For Sale?		
50	YES	NO	MAYBE

Bruce makes his living selling interesting old cars, which is not a very unique business these days. What makes Bruce's business interesting is that, instead of storing his cars in a modern showroom or warehouse, Bruce stores the cars in the vintage Ford dealership he purchased in 1989.

And he lives there with his wife, too!

The building sits in an old section of Staunton which was run down when he bought it. But as the area became gentrified, the building became the centerpiece in the town's beautifully restored historic district.

"This was a Ford dealership from 1911 until 1965, just after the original Mustang was launched," Bruce said as he walked us around the expansive building.

The square footage is actually 27,000 square feet and is comprised of three floors connected by a car elevator. Bruce makes his home on the second floor, in what were the original dealership management offices.

The showroom, which is on the street level, contains a few dozen cars, ranging from a 1957 Cadillac with a camper body installed to the very first 1969 Pontiac GTO Judge to a Richard Petty stock car. These cars are for sale to the general public, and are not what we came here to see. So Bruce led us to the freight elevator for a short ride to the second floor where his real treasures reside.

The first car my eyes focused on was an early Cord sedan.

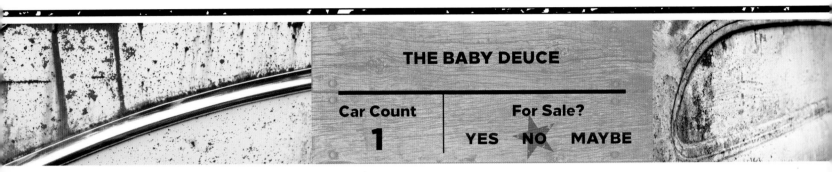

THE BABY DEUCE

Car Count	For Sale?		
1	YES	NO	MAYBE

"That is a supercharged Beverly that is a one-family-owned car," he said of the wonderfully worn but original car. "It was rumored to be in Roanoke for years and nobody could find it. Only 184 supercharged sedans like this were built that year. A buddy of mine got wind of it and tracked it down about four years ago. It has never been touched."

It's upstairs, though, where Bruce stores his seldom-seen cars. This supercharged two-owner, coffin-nose Cord Beverly sedan has spent its entire life within just a few miles of Bruce's dealership.

Bruce said all the upholstery is original and has had only one repaint. The 70,000-mile car is numbers-matching, and he said was only three serial numbers away from the Cord that Ab Jenkins used to set a number of speed records at Bonneville.

"In 1937, this was the Bugatti Veyron of the period, and was considered as a Baby Duesenberg," he said. "The current owner is a doctor, as was the original owner. In order to enhance the car's aerodynamics, the Cord was the first car with hidden headlights, no running boards, and no drip rails. It's at least 9 inches lower in roof height than a Ford of the same year."

Bruce said the motor turns over, but he has not made any attempt to start it.

"You talk about a barn find, most cars of this age would be on its third or fourth upholstery job," he said.

1956 FORD THUNDERBIRD

Car Count	For Sale?
1	YES ★NO MAYBE

"There are lots of 1955, '56, and '57 Thunderbirds that have been restored, but there are none that have one family ownership, original wiring, original paint," said Bruce, as he pulled the car cover off an exceptional T-Bird. "Except this car. This car has 30,000 miles, has the original upholstery, and was purchased from the original owner."

The car is black, has a hardtop with the porthole window, a soft top, and, as with all 1956 Thunderbirds, a Continental Kit. It is powered by a 312-cubic-inch engine with an automatic transmission. The spare tire, jack, and tool kit are all unused.

"This is an unrestored, original car," he said. "And, on the frame rail, there is still the car's stenciled serial number. I've never seen that before. This car has had no rechroming, nothing. It's only had new tires installed."

Bruce also showed us a 1936 Ford Phaeton he is restoring for himself. Interestingly, one of the car's previous owners was a well-known race driver.

"When I bought this car from a friend, he told me that the title still was in the name of a former owner, a Mr. Glen Roberts, better known as Fireball Roberts."

Interesting.

He also showed us a very original 1940 Ford Standard coupe that was not owned by Fireball Roberts, or anyone else famous. "As opposed to every other 1940 Ford coupe in Virginia and North Carolina," he said, "this one did not haul moonshine."

We all laughed as we said our goodnights and headed across the street for a wonderful dinner with Zach and his wife, Brenda.

Day four was an amazing day. In fact, we did not find the most cars that day, but we made the most individual finds so far on our trip.

It was time to call it a night. Back to the Hampton Inn.

Bruce was particularly excited about this '56 T-Bird, a 30,000-mile, one-owner car with original paint, Continental Kit, and like-new interior.

DAY

5

Zach met us at the hotel first thing Tuesday morning. And he brought along an old friend from Long Island whom I hadn't seen in 30 years, Russell Schmidt. Russell was driving a cool 1934 Ford Vicky street rod. We talked Zach and Russell into joining us for breakfast, and he ran a couple of barn-find options past us.

I love waking up in the morning and being given the choice of several old car collections to inspect! One option was the 429 Torino he had told us about the day before, but he noted that we may want to see a couple of other cars first. One was a 1935 Chevy and the other a 1934 Dodge.

Since the Chevy was just a couple of miles away, we opted for that first.

We woke up early, gassed up, and followed friend Zach Strait to several cars that he had lined up for us to see. During our trip, Virginia offered the cheapest gas of the four states we visited.

(top) We followed Zach to his friend Jim Todd's garage. It was early morning, and Michael started to get excited because the sun was shining on Jim's 1935 Chevy sedan just right.

(left) Jim Todd with the Chevy he dragged home from just 1½ miles down the road. It had been purchased new by Jim's uncle. It may be for sale.

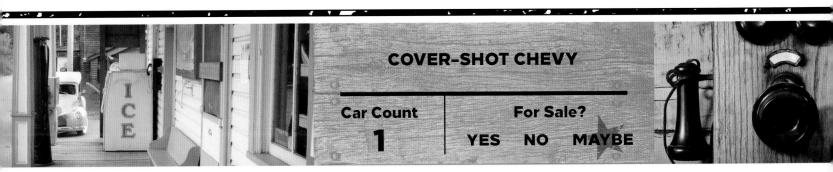

COVER-SHOT CHEVY

Car Count	For Sale?
1	**YES NO MAYBE**

Zach led us to his friend Jim Todd's shop and barn. Inside the barn was a nice old Chevy sedan that got Michael pretty jazzed. You see, our publisher, Zack Miller (Zack with a "k" as opposed to an "h"), kept pressing Michael to look for great front-cover photography for the book. When Michael saw the rustic barn and the way the early morning light was shining on that Chevy, he started to get out his cameras, lenses, and tripods. For a photographer, this was orgasmic stuff!

Meanwhile, Brian and I inspected the car and interviewed the owner.

"I grew up on this farm and today live just over on that hilltop," he said. "The Chevy has been sitting in this barn since 1993. Before I got it, it had been sitting about a mile and a half down the road in the woods. This car was purchased new in 1935 by my great uncle, Wyatt Irvine. This car is called a Master, and is a two-door with a little trunk."

Todd's original plan was to build the Chevy into a street rod, but then his son-in-law expressed interest in it. So it just sits. The car is rough but restorable. It had been originally painted dark green with black fenders.

"Sometime in the 1950s, my great uncle Wyatt sold the car to a guy named Buddy Moore," said Todd. "And I bought the car from Buddy. It was sitting behind his house. When Buddy was done with a car, he just shoved it over into the woods. He also had an old Nash Metropolitan back there. I bought the Chevy for $200."

The Three Stooges of barn finders (from left to right): me, Brian, and Michael. Five days into our adventure, we were holding up pretty well.

Meanwhile, Michael was clicking away with his camera, trying to take advantage of the direct early morning sunlight. The car never looked so good.

Todd couldn't decide whether he would keep the car or sell it, but said he would entertain offers. Upon hearing that, Zach's ears perked up and he said he might be interested in it himself.

Michael completed his photos—one of which is on the cover of this book—and we packed up to see Zach's other friend, Greg Cash, who had an interesting 1934 Dodge just a few miles away.

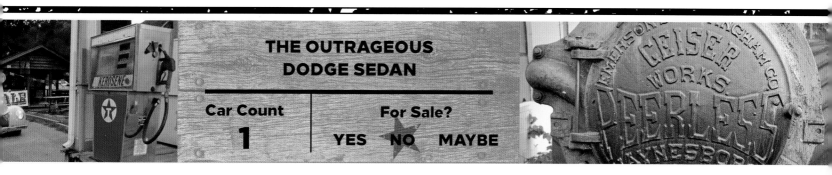

THE OUTRAGEOUS DODGE SEDAN

Car Count	For Sale?		
1	YES	NO	MAYBE

We met Greg at a hodge-podge set of buildings that seemed to have been constructed over a number of years, using a multitude of materials. Greg confirmed that, indeed, the previous owner had been a scavenger who collected odd materials and built this series of structures over time.

And, according to Greg, these rooms we were walking through were at one time so filled with stuff that you couldn't see the opposite wall, which was just 20-feet away! Greg told us that the county came down on the now deceased owner because of all the junk he had piled up in the yard. His "collection" included two old airplanes, which he simply buried in the yard.

Inside the ramshackle building sat a lonely, lovely, 1934 Dodge four-door sedan with just 22,617 miles on the odometer.

"I ate breakfast with the old fellow every morning," said Greg as he explained how he came to own the car. "While he was alive, I never knew he owned the car. When he passed away, his only relatives were a niece and a nephew in Washington State and a niece in Florida.

This Dodge was so well optioned that it was more like a Lincoln or a Cadillac! There has probably never been a better-equipped Dodge.

"I helped them with the estate sale, and they asked me if there was anything I'd personally be interested in, and I said the old car. So after I helped them with all the auctions, they brought me the title and gave me the car. Until he passed away, I didn't even know Neige Deihl had the car."

The car is huge and is probably the most amazing prewar Dodge I've ever seen.

The six-cylinder-powered car had so many options: full wheel covers; artillery wheels; dual generators; an electric pre-selector gearshift (similar to a Cord) with overdrive; four accessory horns; dual side-mount, covered spare tires; accessory trunk on the back; spotlight; turn signals; suitcases; rear heater that circulated hot water from the radiator to the passenger floor; windshield defroster; curb feelers; dual mirrors; accessory bumper guards; rope grab-handles; full sunvisor; and accessory driving lights. It's as though the purchaser ordered every option the dealer had to offer. Or that the Dodge brothers had owned the car themselves.

"This was obviously a high-end car," said Greg. "His cousin told me this car was running just a few years ago."

Full disclosure: I have been a vintage car enthusiast and collector since I was 14 years old, and have always been a Ford man, but this Dodge is one of the most impressive early cars I have ever seen. I have never seen an early car so heavily optioned as this Dodge. It was more Lincoln than Dodge, if that makes any sense.

If it were mine, I would clean it up and enjoy it as is, but Greg would like to restore it back to like-new condition. I know one thing: it will be a very expensive restoration.

Greg said there had also been an Indian motorcycle on the premises that sold during the auction.

"It was all in pieces, and it sold for $4,500," he said. "The guy who bought it sold it for $16,500 on the Internet."

Greg said that he had notified the producers of the American Pickers television program about the impending auction, but they opted not to come.

"I sent them pictures, but they never got back to me," said Greg.

Greg also found a 1927 Harley Davidson motor in all the clutter that sold for $1,200.

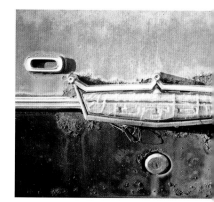

Because Greg doesn't have room for the huge Dodge in his home garage at this time, the deceased man's family told him he could keep it in the building for as long as necessary, or until the real estate is sold.

We had one more stop to make with Zach before he had to go to work and we had to head toward West Virginia.

The Dodge's owner, Greg Cash, hopes to restore the car, which he received as a thank-you for assisting in managing the sale of the estate of the car's longtime owner.

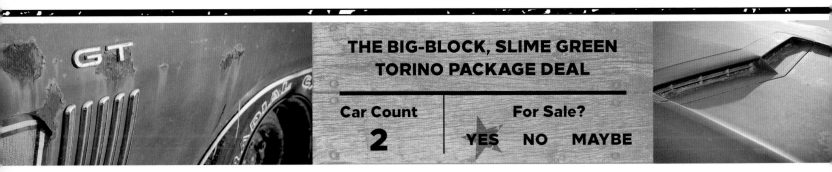

THE BIG-BLOCK, SLIME GREEN TORINO PACKAGE DEAL

Car Count	For Sale?
2	YES NO MAYBE

We followed Zach a few miles away to a former gas station not far from I-81. It is now called Weaver's Garage, and is a truck repair shop. It is run by two brothers, Jim and Steve Weaver. Their late father started the business in 1978.

Sitting on the grass just to the side of the garage was a time-machine 1971 Ford Torino. The car had obviously been sitting in that spot for a long time, because it had sunk into the turf down to its chassis. Next to the Torino was another Ford, a 1966 Galaxie LTD two door, which seems to have been parked there just as long.

This Torino was a muscle car enthusiast's delight: dark green with laser side stripes; 429-cubic-inch engine; four-speed; bench seat; and hideaway headlights. The car had been parked there for at least 20 years, according to Zach. Actually, it was even longer.

"The car has been parked there since 1981 or 1982," said Jim Weaver. "That was the last time Dad put an inspection sticker on it. Now it belongs to both of us."

Their father started to work on the car, but then diabetes started to affect him, so it was parked and it has sat there ever since.

"Dad put on new radial tires and new brakes," said Jim. "He bought it off the original owner."

"And he had a new dual exhaust bent for it like the original system," said Steve Weaver. "It ran pretty strong. The boy that bought it new in 1971 had a friend who bought an identical car except it had a 428-cubic-inch engine in it. One time

This 1971 Ford Torino would have been quite a discovery if it had not spent the last few decades sinking into the turf. The car is an original 429-cubic-inch, four-speed car. I worry about the floorboards and chassis substructure, though.

those two were racing up the interstate, and they were identical in speed until they hit the rest area. That's when the 429 just took off like the 428 was standing still."

The brothers said some work would still be required to get the car complete, like the front bumper would have to be reinstalled, the headliner would have to be replaced, and the four-speed shifter needed to be lubed.

I didn't want to point it out to them, but after sitting outdoors for more than 30 years, the car would need much more work than a bumper installed and a headliner replaced. The car's subframe had been sitting on the grass for decades, so the car's very structure might require major surgery.

From this view, it is obvious that the car is slowly sinking into the earth. The owner has decided to sell the Torino and the LTD as a package deal.

"My dad never bought us anything 'Fireball' like that car, so when he let me drive it, my hair stood straight up on my neck," said Steve. "Then I knew why he never would buy us anything like that."

I asked the brothers how many people have stopped by to ask if the Torino is for sale.

"There ain't a week that goes by that somebody doesn't stop to ask about it," said Steve. "It should have been sold a long time ago."

I spoke to Jim, the older brother, about whether the Torino was for sale.

"I won't split those two cars apart," he said. "I'll only sell the 1966 Galaxie and the Torino together as a package. I've owned that '66 since 1967. It was a good car but not a hot car. It has a 390 in it. I'll take $20,000 for the pair. If the right person were interested in them, they would be a good buy."

I promised Jim and Steve I would keep this Ford package deal in mind for any of my Ford muscle-car friends. We said goodbye and thank-you to Zach, and we headed toward West Virginia.

We had spent too many days in the Roanoke/Staunton area and needed to get into another state to stay on schedule.

"We won't stop again in Virginia, I promise," I said to Brian and Michael.

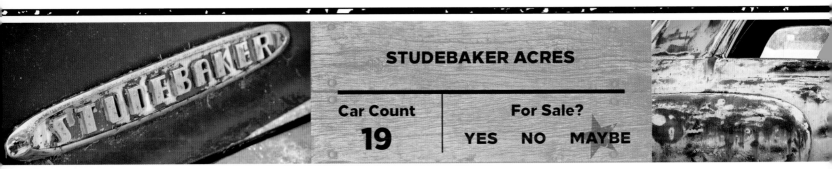

STUDEBAKER ACRES

Car Count	For Sale?
19	YES NO MAYBE

Brian looked at the map and said our best route to West Virginia would be to drive north on State Highway 11 for a few miles before cutting west toward West Virginia. But wouldn't you know, just a few miles up the road from Weaver's Garage we noticed, in the driveway of a very old house, three Studebakers: two pickups, and a sedan.

We had to stop. We just couldn't pass a scene like this.

We made a U-turn in the Woody, Michael following behind in the Ford Flex (I bet we made 500 U-turns on this trip, right, Michael?), and we pulled up in front of that house. I went right up and knocked on the door. No answer. So I walked around to the side door and knocked. No answer there either, although I did disturb a bunch of sleeping cats.

I always recommend knocking on the door before exploring old cars on private property, or else you might be picking buckshot from your hind quarters. Still, I've found that, if you are polite and are genuinely a car person, you can go onto private property without fear of getting arrested. Or shot. At least it hasn't happened to me yet. With nobody at home, as

As we were approaching the West Virginia border, this Studebaker in a driveway got our attention. Little did we know that in the backyard there were a dozen more!

long as we kept our hands in our back pockets, we decided we could probably look around.

Wow, the three Studebakers in the driveway were complimented by a nice old Rambler Super 10 sedan in the front yard. The odometer said only 2,700 miles! Could it be? Then we looked behind the fence in the backyard and couldn't believe what we saw. I counted 15 more Studebaker cars and trucks scattered about.

Darn, I wish somebody were home.

But a few minutes later, a young man came walking from the house. I introduced myself, and he did the same. His name was Adam Early, and he told me that his father, Jerry, owned most of the cars, but that some were also owned by his mother, his brother, and himself.

Adam explained that his family's classic home was built in several phases starting in the 1700s. The first part of the house was a log cabin. "We find pieces of pottery and Civil War coins whenever we dig around here."

Then our conversation turned to old cars.

"My father owned a restoration shop called Early Restorations, and he focused mostly on Studebakers," said Adam, 32. "Then he started restoring Pierce Arrows. Now he is retired, but we've been into Studebakers for a long time."

Adam explained that most of the cars we were looking at were purchased as parts cars, and that his family stored their nicer cars in a nearby warehouse.

Adam also told me that the Rambler I had been admiring in his front yard does in fact have less than 3,000 miles on the odometer, and had never even had an oil change until they bought it. And the spare tire has never been mounted. It had been discovered in a shed in Staunton, where it had been parked for 30 years. It is now his mother's car.

It's a family affair: Jerry, Adam, and Betty Early pose next to one of the many Studebakers in their backyard.

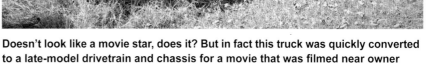

Doesn't look like a movie star, does it? But in fact this truck was quickly converted to a late-model drivetrain and chassis for a movie that was filmed near owner Jerry Early's house.

Hiding behind the hedge in the front yard is probably the lowest-mileage 1959 Rambler 10 in existence. Just 2,700 miles are registered on the odometer, and the spare tire is brand new.

As we were talking, a car pulled into the driveway and two folks approached us. Walking toward us were Jerry and Betty Early, Adam's parents. Adam introduced us to his parents and said that some of their cars were for sale.

"Well, actually, if you ask my dad, none of the cars are for sale, but if you ask my mom, they are all for sale," he said. "If you ask me, it depends.

"The only car I won't sell is the Rambler, because the first song I heard when I turned on the radio was, 'Oh, Elizabeth' by the Statler Brothers," said Betty. "That's my name."

Adam's dad pointed to one of the pickup trucks in the driveway and told us it was a 1992 Studebaker. I wondered what he meant.

"That truck was in a movie," he said. "*Hearts in Atlantis,* a Castle Rock production that was filmed right here in Staunton. The movie people pulled up and asked if we had any cars they could rent. I worked on that project for two weeks. It's sitting on a Jeep Wagoneer chassis, four-wheel-drive and everything."

The family has lived in this house for 40 years, but they have been into Studebakers even longer.

"I drove one back in college," said Jerry. "A 1956 President."

This was a happy family, and the perfect way to end our barn-finding in the state of Virginia. We will not stop again until we are out of this state!

It occurred to me that I could probably write a book exclusively about the old cars in the state of Virginia. I mean, we had discovered dozens of cars just within the Roanoke area, and there were plenty of towns and villages between there and the coast.

Virginia had been good to us, and we were now officially saying goodbye to this bountiful state.

As we were sprinting toward West Virginia, this Chevy and Plymouth on the right side of the road got our attention. These two cars led us to 40 more.

—— OMG, WE NEED TO STOP! ——

I swear we intended to leave the state, driving west toward West Virginia—purposely not looking left or right—until…

"Stop!" Brian shouted.

We had just passed a bunch of old cars, cars in fields, cars in sheds, and cars in barns. Another incredible Virginia discovery.

HORTON'S BARN-FIND HEAVEN

Car Count	For Sale?
42	YES NO MAYBE

We made yet another U-turn and doubled back a couple of hundred feet to inspect what we had stumbled across. I'll bet Junior Johnson never made as many bootleg turns as we did, even in his moonshining days!

This was not a happenchance assembly of vehicles; this was one heck of a collection of 1950s and 1960s cars. A quick survey revealed that the owner had an eclectic taste. I knocked on the door of the farmhouse, but nobody was home. So we figured we could walk around with our hands in our pockets again and look without offending anyone.

Thankfully many of the cars in Robert Horton's collection are under cover, which has kept cars like this Edsel in solid condition.

A Hudson and a Rambler huddle next to one another under the tin-roof shed. Robert said that he would consider selling some of his collection.

Out in the field were about a dozen cars, including this 1963 Mercury Monterey and a 1960 Lancer, the Dodge version of the Plymouth Valiant.

We were just beginning to check out this cache when a man came riding up on a four-wheeler. I figured he was the owner. He wasn't. His name was Mike Zimmerman, and he was a neighbor and friend of the cars' owner.

"I live across the field, and saw some people walking around Robert's house," said Mike. "I didn't think he was expecting any visitors, so I figured I better check out who it was."

Mike was a cool guy and proudly told us he owned three 1961 Ford Starliners: one that was owned by his late father, one he bought, and another parts car. He had no problem with us walking around looking at his neighbor's cars. He told us the cars belonged to his friend, Robert Horton.

Ok, ready? Here is what Mr. Horton had parked on his property (in no particular order): Hudsons, Fraziers, Mercurys (Montclairs and Comets), a Willys, a Crosley, a Ford Fairlane, Studebakers, Nashes (including Metropolitans), Plymouths (Valiants and otherwise), Ramblers, a VW Beetle, Edsels, Chevys, Fords, a Rambler Cross Country wagon complete with a Pininfarina-designed body, and a steam engine.

Steam engine?

Yes, a 1914 Kaiser Peerless Steam Engine, complete with huge steel wheels, that Mike showed had current license tags. He said it had been

A former chicken coop housed the nicest cars in Robert's collection, including Fords, Ramblers, Hudsons, Nash Metropolitans, T-Birds, and others.

recently driven for a parade. Its owner told me later it is 100 years old, and back in the day it was a power unit.

"It could be used as a tractor, a saw mill, or it could pull a gang of mowers or plows," he said.

Mike told us that Robert was currently at the Carlisle flea market and would be going directly to Hershey immediately afterward. He did offer to get Robert on the phone, which we greatly appreciated.

Robert proved to be an interesting guy. We spoke for a few moments on the phone, then I interviewed him at Hershey the following week. This is what I learned:

"I've been collecting cars my whole life," he said. "I got my first car when I was 12 years old. It was a 1940 Pontiac that was sitting at a woman's yard up the street. She asked, 'Would you like to have it?' It took a while to convince my father, but he finally said yes, so he helped me tow it home behind his tractor."

Robert makes his living as shop manager at WW Motorcars and Parts, a restoration shop where he has worked for 23 years.

"Even though I work on old cars every day, it's still just a hobby," he said.

I asked if any of his cars are for sale.

"Some are for sale, and some I'll keep," he said. "Unless I was offered a ridiculous amount of money—then everything is for sale."

Brian already had designs on buying a 1963 Mercury Monterey two-door from Robert, which he thought would look just right slammed to the ground, with dual exhaust and some kind of funky wheel/tire package. Now remember, he had fallen in love with A. C. Wilson's Lincoln Continental just a day or two earlier. I'm beginning to think that falling in love is a daily routine for my navigator.

Some of the prettiest roads we encountered were on the border between Virginia and West Virginia.

—— WESTWARD HO! ——

Well, that discovery provided a terrific climax to the great state of Virginia. As we swiftly drove west toward West Virginia, I told Brian, "I don't care if we pass a Duesenberg in the bushes, we're not going to stop."

And true to our words, we kept on trucking, not past Duesenbergs, but lots of old Ford and Chevy pickup trucks and sedans, and even a street rod shop. There were cars that we would have normally stopped and photographed, but not now. I had budgeted three to four days per state, and we needed to leave Virginia or we'd blow our schedule.

Finally, we crossed the West Virginia state line, and to celebrate, we stopped at a very old and authentic general store for an RC Cola and a Moon Pie.

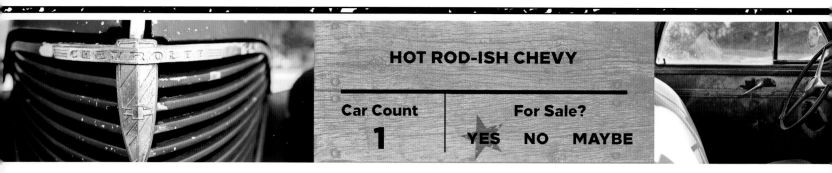

HOT ROD-ISH CHEVY

Car Count	For Sale?		
1	YES	NO	MAYBE

Almost immediately after crossing into West Virginia, we passed an old Chevy coupe. It turned out to be a 1939 Chevy that had been modified with a Nova sub-frame and a 305-cubic-inch engine. The car was for sale and included $1,000 worth of new red paint in the can and a new battery. It would be an easy project to complete for someone with minimal mechanical skills and a moderately equipped shop. The owner was not at home, so we spoke to his uncle, who didn't know all the details.

For the next hour or so, we drove through some of the most beautiful countryside we would see during our two-week journey. We drove through a rural valley between two mountain ranges, the sun was shining, the weather was warm, and the scenery was spectacular. The terrain kept changing but was constantly beautiful.

As we crossed a second set of mountains, we came to a wide spot in the road that held a site that made us weak.

No, we didn't see a field full of old cars, but a rusty, very old commercial, tin-sided building. On the building was a sign that read Seneca Motor Company. Next to it was an old neon Ford Tractor sign. This was a must-stop situation.

We parked the Woody in front of the building, and as we were snooping around, two gentlemen came driving up. "We'll have to charge you if you take photos of that building," one of them said. They looked serious, then they both smiled. They were cousins and explained that their grandfather had opened Seneca Motor Company,

Michael shoots a selfie after downing an RC Cola and a Moon Pie at a countryside general store. That's a classic road trip lunch, Michael!

Soon after finally crossing into West Virginia, we came across this 1939 Chevy coupe that had been modified with a V-8. It was not completed and was for sale.

the Ford car, truck, and tractor dealership of Seneca Rocks, West Virginia, back in 1915.

One of the men, Joe Harper, smoked a stogie and told us he owned 3,500 acres where he raises sheep and cuts timber. Joe also owns the adjacent general store and restaurant and suggested we try the lamb for dinner if we didn't have any other plans.

"This road here was dirt and ran through the valley when my grandfather opened his store," Joe said. "And no people lived on it."

He said, though, that anyone within miles would come to buy cars from their grandfather. The dealership is long closed, but the grand, old building remains.

We took Joe's advice and all three of us tried the lamb dinner—delicious—and enjoyed some local West Virginia craft beer and spent time talking to Joe about the history of the area. He said that the mountain opposite his store attracts hikers and climbers from all over the country. He said that many folks are naïve, thinking the climb is a simple one. But he said people have fallen to their death trying to get to that peak.

Fortunately neither Brian, Michael, nor I planned on climbing that peak this evening, so we said goodbye and continued down what was once a dirt road.

The sun was going down and we needed to find a place to rest our heads for the night.

We stayed in a Hampton Inn in Elkins, West Virginia. Nothing unusual, except that the next morning we'd find out that we had luckily chosen just the right Hampton Inn.

This scenic overlook in West Virginia's Germany Valley was too good a photo op to ignore.

Seneca Motor Company in Seneca Rocks, West Virginia, was a Ford car, truck, and tractor dealership that opened in 1915 and closed in the 1960s.

DAY

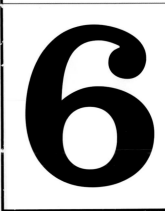

6

We preferred staying in Hampton Inns for several reasons: the rooms are clean, breakfast is free, and they almost always allowed us to park the Woody under the front entrance canopy to keep it out of the weather and rain. But this Hampton Inn offered another benefit that we would discover while eating breakfast.

I decided to get up early and go running for a few miles, hoping to wear off some of that beer and beef I had been consuming nightly. Plus, in the past, I've discovered quite a few cars while pounding pavement on an early morning jog.

But this time, I found none. As far as I could tell, Elkin was barren of old cars. At least that's what I thought…

Cindy Phares, who works at the Elkins, West Virginia, Hampton Inn, approached us and said she had an old car at her house. This 1959 Plymouth Savoy has lived within a mile of Cindy's house its whole life.

(top) When Cindy traded her husband's BSA motorcycle for the Savoy, she had the local vo-tech high school restore the body and apply new paint.

(left) Cindy's dog, Meatwad, guards her husband's '64 Chevy Impala. Down, Meatwad!

Brian was woofing down his high-protein breakfast of eggs and bacon, Michael had cereal and pastry, and I mostly had yogurt and fruit. As we were sitting there, munching, the woman who worked in the Hampton Inn breakfast room approached us.

"Are you the guys with the Woody?" she asked.

"Yes, but how could you tell?" I asked.

"Well I saw the faces on the decal, and you are the only ones in here that looked like them," she said.

She introduced herself as Cindy Phares, and she said she owned an old Plymouth that was sitting in her yard just a few miles away.

"If you'd like to see it, I get off work in a little while," she said.

—— THE LOCAL PLYMOUTH SAVOY ——

We cruised through town looking for cars while waiting for Cindy to get off work at 10:00 a.m. Then we followed her over the river and through the woods to her house in the rural West Virginia countryside.

There sat a wonderfully nostalgic Plymouth Savoy sedan, a powder blue version of the movie car in *Christine*.

"It has a three on the column," Cindy said as she showed us her car. "You know that red house we passed on the way here?" she asked. I did remember passing a red house about ¼ mile back. "The man who lives there now is named Virgil. His daddy bought this car brand-new in 1959.

"It only has 45,000 miles on it. I suspect he only drove it to town on Sundays. He never took it out of town, as far as I know. Then his son, Virgil, who is now 84, had it for years. Then my brother-in-law, who lives in the farmhouse across the creek, got the car. He left it out in the field to rust. So when I found out it was a '59, and I was born in '59, I had to have it."

Ever since the car was bought new in 1959, it had been owned by four different owners—who all lived within a half-mile from where we were standing. Amazing.

Cindy wanted the car, so she traded her husband's 1960-something BSA motorcycle to her brother-in-law for the Plymouth. Her brother-in-law still has the BSA, which he has never even ridden.

Cindy is surrounded by "kin." Her husband and all his brothers were born in the family farmhouse just over the creek. There were 13 kids altogether, who were all raised on the 250-acre spread.

"They paid $3,000 or $4,000 for the land, and the family did some farming," she said.

"I wanted the Plymouth to drive," said Cindy. "I got the local vo-tech school to do the bodywork and paint on the car, and the next step was to do the interior. I know it needs brake lines and new tires. But it runs well."

But then she mentioned she would sell it.

"I know it will never get finished. My husband has his own Chevy projects he's working on. I'm thinking $4,000 would be a fair price."

She showed us a couple of cars her husband and her son own: a 1964 Impala and a 1972 Monte Carlo. As we were walking around inspecting her family's cars, we were accompanied by her dog, who had the wonderful name of Meatwad. Really.

"If it was up to me, I'd sell these two cars, because I don't think they'll ever get fixed," she said of the two Chevys. "But they will probably sit here forever."

We followed Cindy to her brother-in-law's house up the hill. She thought we might like to see his collection of old motorcycles.

Cindy's brother-in-law, Dick, lives just up the road from the house where he was born. His garage and sheds are littered with numerous BSA, Triumph, and Harley motorcycles. None are for sale.

Old Rider

"My first bike was a 125cc BSA," said Cindy's brother-in-law, Dick Phares. "Then I got a 250cc BSA when I went to California. I've been through a lot of them since."

Today, Dick owns a Harley with a '55 engine on a later model frame with later wheels. "Those hard tails would kill you," he said. So he built a vintage-looking Softtail for himself.

Even though he is 71 years old, and admittedly running out of energy, he said that none of his bikes were for sale. He showed us a racing Triumph Rickman, which was sitting in a lean-to behind

En route to Morgantown, West Virginia, we saw this mothballed locomotive. The 1950 GM has 2,250 horsepower.

his garage. He also had three BSA 441s that he hoped to turn into one decent bike someday.

"But you know, I kind of like those electric starts these days," said Dick.

Inside he had several late 1960s, early 1970s Triumphs.

"It's awful when you have so many bikes you can't remember what year they are," Dick said.

We thanked Cindy for introducing herself at the Hampton Inn, and said good-bye. We began to drive toward Morgantown, where we would spend the night. We had heard about Morganton Brewing Company and thought that it might be a neat place to have dinner and talk with some of the locals.

En route to Morgantown, we passed an old train graveyard, and we had to stop.

Brian, our heavy equipment specialist, was salivating at the sight of the old steam and diesel locomotives, especially the ones with art deco styling. In the yard was a GM-EMD E-8A. Fascinated, Brian texted his buddy and train enthusiast Rob Maloney for more information. Within an hour we found out that Engine #92 was delivered to the Baltimore & Ohio Railroad in 1950, finished in the beautiful Baltimore & Ohio blue, gray, and black Capitol Dome paint scheme. This passenger road locomotive was in service for B&O before becoming Amtrak locomotive #210. Ultimately it ended up in the collection of the Baltimore & Ohio Railroad Museum before finding its way to this resting place in Elkins, West Virginia.

It seemed Day 6 would not be such a great day for discovering cars. Even though we had driven beautiful rural roads for several hours, we had not made any great finds. Little did we know that, as the sun began to set, we'd stumble onto a wonderful discovery.

We were following our GPS directions to the brewery, which was in Morgantown. But the turn came up too quickly, so we had to go past it a couple of blocks and make yet another U-turn. As we doubled back toward the brewery, less than 100 feet from where we would turn right into the brewery's parking lot, I noticed an old garage door in a commercial building. The door was open and a 1941 Ford was peeking out.

Could it be that just a half-a-block from the brewery we had made the discovery of another car? It turned out better than that. We pulled our Woody and the Flex into Morgantown Brewing Company's small parking lot in the back of their building. Then we walked directly back to the old garage to have a look.

The interior of the building was littered with old cars.

This is the former Morgantown Chevrolet dealership, now home of Vic's Towing. When we drove by, I noticed a surprise sitting inside the open garage door.

BARN FINDS IN THE CITY

Car Count	For Sale?		
11	YES	NO	MAYBE

I saw a woman in the office and asked her about the cars.

"They belong to my brother Vic," said Cindy Solomon. "You can have a look around if you like."

Vic Solomon operated Vic's Towing Service, a business his father started decades earlier. Even though many of the cars he had stored were newer—a Firebird and a couple of Camaros that were not particularly interesting to me—a number of the cars were genuine barn finds.

Looking for Morgantown Brewery, I saw this 1941 Ford peeking out of an old garage in the middle of town, and just 200 feet from the brewery!

We walked through the garage, and in addition to the '41 Ford two-door sedan, we saw a 1937 Packard sedan and a 1939 Mercury sedan. These cars were all in very nice condition but were absolutely filthy and obviously neglected.

Cindy told us the building used to be a Chevy dealership, which made sense, because there was a spiral ramp in the back that led to a second floor. It was too tempting to pass up, so we hiked the steep incline and discovered another stash of old metal.

The building was obviously in need of major repair because there were puddles of rainwater on the floor. And there were a number of old cars sitting among those puddles. Here was a 1938 Ford four-door sedan, an Edsel, and a '47 Pontiac.

As we were snooping around, owner Vic Solomon arrived back. He was a dead-ringer for actor Peter Falk. Vic explained that the building had once been home to Wilson Chevrolet. He said their body shop was located upstairs, showroom on the street level, and mechanical repairs in the basement. We walked around with Vic and asked him to tell us about some of the old cars he owned. He started with the 1938 Ford Deluxe four-door, which he said was rust-free.

Wedged between a Packard and an XJ6 Jaguar was this 1939 Mercury two-door sedan. The car, which belongs to Vic Solomon, is remarkably clean because it is kept covered.

"If you lift up the floor mats in that car, the paint on the floorboards are just as shiny as when it was new," he said. "It has been off the road since World War II and only has 48,000 miles. The old fellow kept it because he thought his son was coming home from the war, but he had been killed. So when the old fellow died, we bought it at an auction. I've had it since the early '70s."

Vic said he has owned the 1941 Ford since the early 1970s as well. The last time it ran was when he bought it. I asked if he had restored it, and Vic said no, he had bought it in this condition. It was pretty nice.

He explained that he and his father once operated a full-service repair shop, but when cars became more complicated, they decided not to invest in the necessary new equipment. So these days, he just stores cars and operates his towing service.

"My brother bought the 1937 Packard from the local Subaru dealer," said Vic. "When the dealer filed bankruptcy, he bought the car at auction about three years ago."

Next to the Packard was a 1939 Mercury, which is a very rare car because it was the first year of Mercury production.

"My buddy found that car on the computer," said Vic. "The old guy was selling out of everything and moving to

This '37 Packard belongs to Vic's brother. It is coated in dust and serves as a superhighway for a resident cat and a visiting raccoon.

The second floor of Vic's Towing held some real gems. This 1938 Ford four-door sedan is particularly clean. The paint on the rear floor still shines!

Florida. I suppose it has been restored at one time, but I just don't know. It has 22,000 miles on it. I bought it because I was never going to find another one."

Many of the cars had huge raccoon foot prints in the dust that rested on all the horizontal surfaces. He said the raccoon comes into his garage every night, probably through one of the missing windows panes.

Next to the '38 Ford upstairs were a bunch of other cars: a 1947 Buick fastback; '65 Ford Galaxy convertible; a Nash Metropolitan with 22,000 miles; a 1919 Ford Model T Depot Hack that had been owned by a local oil company; an Edsel with a shifter in the steering wheel; and several others. I asked Vic if he would sell any of these cars.

"I'm going to start selling this stuff next year," he said. "I'm 65 years old now, and in January I'll be 66. I told my sister I wanted to quit then."

Vic told us his family also owns a junkyard outside of town. His father started it in 1945, but most of the old cars in their junkyard had been crushed years ago when the price of scrap metal was high. He did invite us to visit the junkyard but warned us that most of the old cars were very rusty. We decided to pass on the offer.

A local oil company originally owned this Model T Ford truck. The Edsel next door has push-button shifting in the center of the horn button.

This 1967 Ford convertible is a low-rider because of the flat tires. The 289-powered car would be a snap to restore.

Wow, what an evening. It seems that whenever we begin to get depressed that we haven't found enough cars, around the next corner we stumble on anther stash!

So it was on to Morgantown Brewing Company for some food and libations, and maybe some more leads. Jesse Sedlock, the brewmaster, and Dina Brewer (perfect name, right?), our bartender, made us feel right at home. I had the Pale Ale and the IPA, which, along with a cheeseburger, made an ideal meal at the end of a great day.

While we were eating, we began chatting with several patrons who were fascinated by our adventure. It seems that we were living out many people's fantasies of just taking off on a road trip with no time schedule or destination.

Vic Solomon is surrounded by at least 11 special-interest cars at his Morgantown towing service. He has hundreds of less interesting cars.

Vic's personal favorite is this 1947 Buick two-door fastback sedan. All these cars are under cover, but all the protective roofs' leaks mean the cars often sit in puddles.

DAY

Hump Day! We're half-way through our 14-day journey!

We stopped back at Vic Solomon's one more time to take additional photos in the daylight and to say goodbye to Vic and his sister, Cindy. They had been so accommodating to allow us full access to their building.

We had driven about 1,100 miles so far, not quite halfway into our adventure. Even though we had hoped to spend much more time in West Virginia, we started to plan our escape toward Maryland. This is too bad, because I have never spent much time in the Mountain State, even though I do love it for its scenery. But, because we spent too many days in Virginia, we needed to start heading for our third state, Maryland.

Brian was planning the next leg of our journey, which would take us slightly north and east, still trying to stay exclusively on secondary roads.

—— HEY, OFFICER... ——

We drove eastbound on Highway 7 in West Virginia, towards Hagerstown, Maryland, and stopped for lunch at a family-style restaurant. A Preston County sheriff was eating lunch, too, so I walked over to talk to him.

"Excuse me, sir, but my friends and I are riding around looking for old cars that may be in the area," I said. "Because you get all around the county on back roads, might you know of any old cars around here on farms or behind houses?"

He was not very encouraging.

"A few years ago, we had a big junk drive in the county to clean up the area," said the sheriff. "Most of the old cars were hauled to the scrap yard and crushed."

Oh, shucks, I didn't want to hear that.

Back on the road on Highway 7, we were just a few miles from the restaurant when we spotted an old Ford in a driveway on the left side. From the road, it appeared to be either a 1955 or '56 Ford.

(top) This 1956 Ford Crown Victoria sits in the West Virginia driveway of Huey Roberts, who is restoring it for his sister, Pam.

(left) No road trip is complete without your vehicle breaking down. Brian and I had to make some field repairs on the Woody—we installed a shorter drive belt to bypass a seized a/c compressor.

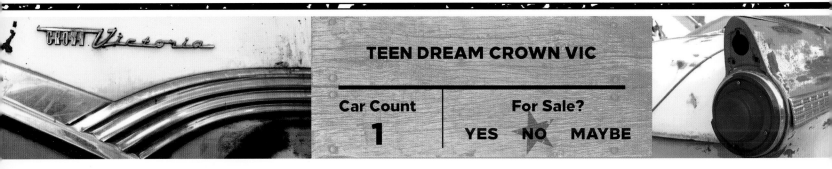

TEEN DREAM CROWN VIC

Car Count	For Sale?
1	**YES NO MAYBE**

We turned into the driveway to have a closer look. A man who was standing there greeted us. His name was Huey Roberts.

I told him we were looking for old cars, and would he mind talking with us about his old Ford. The car was partially covered, so I wasn't quite sure which body style it was.

"It's a '56 Crown Victoria," said Huey. "It belongs to my sister, Pam. I'm going to restore the car for her."

The car was pretty solid, and partially disassembled. I called Pam, who lives in Newport, Tennessee, and asked her about the car.

"My father-in-law, Bud, has owned two Crown Victorias since he was in his 20s," Pam said. "One of them has the glass top. He finally decided that he was never going to restore both of them, so he gave one to his son, my husband, Tony. We're having the car restored in its original pink and white paint job and will give it to my daughter, Page, who is 15 years old. She'll drive it to high school."

Pam mentioned her father-in-law had another old vehicle at his home in Tennessee, a 1953 Chevy five-window pickup truck.

"Bud gave that to Tony, who will fix it up and give it to my nine-year-old son, Harley."

Pam grew up in the West Virginia Mountains but moved when she got married. I asked her if there were any old cars near where she lives now.

Brian and I strategizing on how to remedy the seized air conditioner compressor issue. Use of a smaller belt eliminated the a/c unit but would cause another issue two days later.

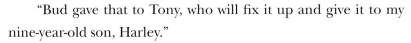

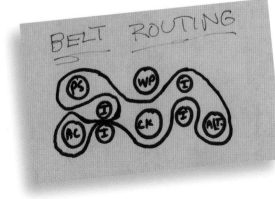

"There are antique cars all over the place around here," she said. "But nobody sells anything. They'd rather just let them rust into the ground."

Unfortunately, we've all heard those stories too many times. I told Pam that if we ever write another *Barn Find Road Trip* book, we'd definitely consider checking out her area in Tennessee.

Soon after crossing into Maryland, the Woody started to give us a problem. At first I heard an irritating squeak. Then there was a smoky smell.

At a traffic light, smoke wafted up from under the hood. It was time to pull over and see what was going on.

Yuck! The smell of burning rubber when I opened the hood was pretty awful. I realized that something was going on with the rubber serpentine belt. Once I started the engine, it became apparent that the air conditioning compressor pulley was not spinning, obviously seized. Thank goodness we were in a small town that had a couple of auto parts stores.

We limped the car to one of the local stores and appraised our options.

Brian and I decided that if we were able to install a smaller belt, we could eliminate the air conditioning compressor altogether. Thankfully, the folks in the store agreed to allow us to test fit a number of belts before purchasing.

Thankfully we made it to an auto parts store where they let us test fit several belts.

Brian dove underneath the Woody, and I worked on the top side. We removed the serpentine belt and began the custom-fitting process. After 20 minutes of trial-and-error test fittings, we decided on a belt of the correct length. This wasn't a repair job with the speed of a NASCAR pit stop, but at least we got back onto the road without too much drama.

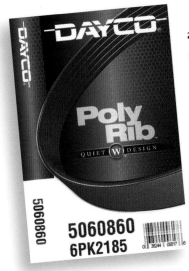

Success!

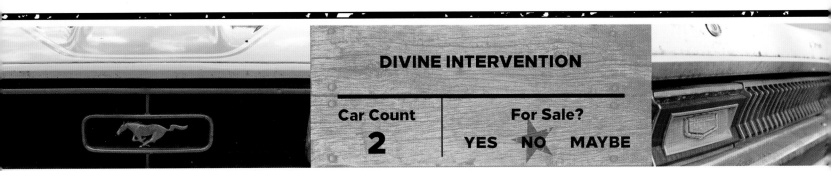

DIVINE INTERVENTION

Car Count	For Sale?
2	YES NO MAYBE

A few more miles down the road and we were in an area where we could drive back and forth between West Virginia and Maryland, the state line was that well defined. We drove into West Virginia for a few minutes, but that town did not seem to hold any automotive treasures. So we crossed back into Westernport, Maryland, and for some reason I felt compelled to drive down one particular road.

Whether you believe in a Greater Being or not, I felt attracted to a church that sat in the middle of a residential area. And son of a gun, in the church parking lot were two old cars, a 1969 Mercury Cougar and a 1971 Mustang Mach 1. Who would've thunk it? I knocked on the door of what appeared to be the preacher's house, and a young woman came to the door. I asked about the cars.

"Those are my father's," said Christa Hammond. "His name is Greg, and he is the minister. It's the First Assembly of God, a Pentecostal church."

Christa came out to the parking lot to show us her dad's cars. Accompanying Christa were her two sons, who had 600 horsepower of energy! The boys names

In a case of divine intervention, we were mysteriously led down a certain street in Westernport, Maryland, to discover these two muscle cars in a church parking lot.

were Austin, who was six, and Cooper, who was four. Christa's hands were certainly full with these two young guys.

Austin and Cooper... seems there was an automotive influence when they were named...

"My father was a mechanic for most of his life," said Christa. "His occupation is mechanic, but his calling is the ministry. But he's always loved old cars. When he was 16 years old, he had a Mach 1 Mustang. He's in his mid-50s now. I know he'd like to repaint the Mustang red metalflake."

Turns out that Pastor Greg Hammond loves to soup up cars and burn rubber! He has great plans for the Mach 1 and Cougar.

After the trip, I was able to interview Christa's father Greg on the telephone. Before joining the ministry, Greg and his father had an auto repair shop. Then he worked at a Chrysler dealership for 20 years.

"I bought the Cougar from a friend," said Greg, who has been a minister for 20 years, 10 in the town of Westernport, Md. "He had originally bought it as a gift for his girlfriend, but she was cheating on him, so he sold the car to me for $2,000. It's a sleeper; it has a 351 Windsor with about 400 horsepower, but I'm thinking about installing a big-block in it with a four-speed."

He said he's already burned out two automatic transmissions because he likes to power-brake. This is one hip minister!

Soon after acquiring the Cougar, he was on a pastoral visit to a woman's home and noticed a Mustang Mach 1 in her yard.

"It belonged to her daughter, and she had an attachment to it," he said. "She said if she decided to sell it, she'd call me first. Well, about 10 years go by, and I forgot about it, when she called me. I bought it for $2,000 as well."

No word on whether Greg runs holy water in his cooling system!

He plans on restoring the Mach 1, although the engine will be modified.

"It's not in my DNA to leave engines stock," said Greg.

One thing Greg misses most is a garage to work in.

"I need to find one before I start modifying the Cougar," he said. "I once fixed up and painted a pickup truck in the church parking lot. Never again."

It was nice to see a man of the cloth who was able to maintain his love of muscle cars.

PRETTY SPECIAL BUICK SPECIAL

Car Count	For Sale?
1	YES NO MAYBE

Just a few minutes after leaving the Hammonds', we passed a very cool looking old Buick. I had to stop. It was so art deco, red and white and just looked so period correct.

I knocked on the door and asked about the car. The man who answered said it was his son's car. It was a 1953 two-door hardtop, and his son's wife's uncle gave it to them.

"I bought it with my income tax return check," Milburn Viler Jr. said. "It runs good. I'm going to put it on the road and take it to some shows around town this summer.

"A woman has already asked me if she could use it for her daughter's wedding!"

—— DINNER AT UNCLE JACKS ——

We checked into another Hampton Inn in Frostburg, Maryland, and asked the desk clerk where he would recommend we have dinner. He said there were a number of restaurants in the area—TGIF, Applebee's, etc.—just a mile away.

I told him we were not big fans of franchise restaurants, and asked where we might find a nice pub in a downtown setting. He recommended traveling east to Cumberland, about 30 minutes away. That was a little bit further than we would have liked, but who knows; we might get a good lead on our next old car discovery from one of the locals.

Just a couple of miles from Pastor Hammond's church, we came across Milburn Viler's 1953 Buick two-door hardtop. There was just something about the look of this car that attracted us to it.

So we climbed into the Woody and drove to Cumberland. We cruised around until we found Uncle Jack's Pizzeria & Pub. We took our place at the bar and ordered a few local beers and pizza. (Boy, did we eat a lot of pizza on this trip!)

We started chatting with some of the other patrons. One guy told us of an abandoned house in nearby Short Gap, West Virginia. He said there were a bunch of old cars, including an old Porsche and an old Saab.

"It's right off Knobbly Road, on Dirty Foot Road," he said. "It's the house on the right. The guy who lived there died, and they want to sell everything."

Wow, what a deal. We thanked him for the lead and told him we'd check it out in the morning.

The bartender overheard our conversation. She introduced herself as Amy Turner, at which point all three of us started to sing "Amy," the old Pure Prairie League tune.

"That's my favorite song," she said. "I never get tired of hearing it.

"I've lived here my whole life. I grew up in a junkyard and a used car lot. But my father died in 1988, and now there is nothing left."

We had a great pizza, said good-bye to Amy and her co-workers, and fired the Woody up for our 30-minute drive back to Frostburg. We already had a lead for tomorrow.

Amy, our bartender at Uncle Jacks, wanted to see the car that was causing all the excitement inside the pub!

DAY

We started our adventure last Friday, so this is the beginning of our second week on the road. We're still having fun (at least I am), and so far Brian's and Michael's snoring has not kept me awake too much.

First thing we wanted to check out was the West Virginia lead we got last night at Uncle Jack's. When Brian and I heard there was an old Porsche, we both began to imagine that perhaps it would be an RSR, or a Spyder, or maybe a Turbo race car. Or at the very least, an early, non-rusty 911.

We used our Atlas and GPS to find our way to Knobbly Road, and then Dirty Foot Road. This was rural West Virginia, and street signs were not too helpful, but eventually we found the house.

We were disappointed.

Yes, there was a Porsche, a very nice 944. The Saab: a late model. There were a couple of other cars, like a couple of 1990s Chryslers, but nothing that fit our

description of a barn find. So much for finding a vintage Porsche 356 with a four-cam Carrera engine, and maybe a nice, old Saab with a three-cylinder, two-stroke engine. Oh, well, the definition of "old car" is not the same for everyone.

This find did not meet our high standards.

As we were leaving Dirty Foot Road, we noticed two old cars, one in a driveway and one behind the house—a Buick and a Cadillac. I knocked on the door and met Cheryl Fields. She and (top) Cheryl and David Fields of Short Gap, West Virginia, have a couple of cool rides running, and another one in construction. This 1946 Buick has a 383 stroker engine and troublesome Jaguar headlights.

(left) The Fields bought this 1942 Cadillac as an original car for $1,200 and installed a 500-cubic-inch Caddy engine and disc brakes. They have driven the car to many street rod meets. Their 1947 Chevy panel is still under construction.

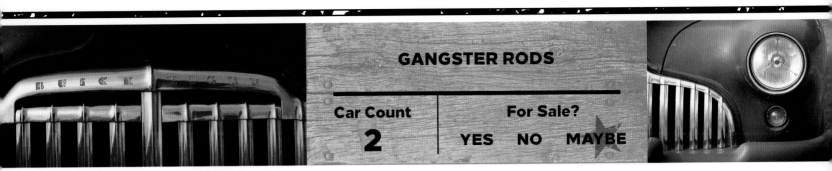

GANGSTER RODS

Car Count	For Sale?
2	YES NO MAYBE

ALMOST HEAVEN, WEST VIRGINIA

We weren't trying to spend more time in West Virginia, it's just that the Maryland/Virginia/West Virginia state lines were so close to each other in this area that we crisscrossed from state to state without even realizing it.

That, and there are just so many old cars in West Virginia. It seemed that no matter what road we drove down, we stumbled across vintage tin.

Another thing: when we asked car folks in Virginia or Maryland about where old cars could be found, they said, "There are no old cars around here anymore." But when we asked West Virginians about old cars, they said, "There are plenty all over the state." In fact, most people were saddened by their state's beautification programs that were responsible for entire junkyards being crushed.

It seems that old cars are an accepted form of yard art in West Virginia. Plus folks just enjoy tinkering with old machines, whether they are cars, trucks, tractors, or whatever. There is a real appreciation for vehicles that were built to be serviced by the owner.

her husband, David, live in Short Gap, West Virginia, and own these two flat-black hot rods.

"We found the Cadillac in a barn," she said. "The guy needed to move it because he ran out of room. It had the original flathead eight cylinder in it when we bought it. Now it has a 1977 500 [cubic-inch Caddy] engine and disc brakes. It's a 1942, and one of the last 100 Cadillacs built before passenger-car production ended before World War II."

The car had been in Burlington, West Virginia. Cheryl and David saw a note posted about the Caddy limo at a car show in Altoona, Pennsylvania.

"The man who was selling it said, 'I have to get my money out of it,' so I asked, 'How much is that?' And he said, '$1,200,'" said Cheryl. "We thought he might want $5,000 for it, because it ran. We've had it for 12 years and it runs well. We did the work ourselves."

The Buick also had an interesting history.

"The Buick is a 1946, and was one of the first 200 to be built after the war," she said. "It has a Fleetwood body as well. It has a 383 Chevy stroker engine."

Cheryl said they bought the car about eight or nine years ago from a friend. It had a purple paint job when they bought it.

"The Buick had 1977 Jaguar headlights, but I couldn't find new bulbs, so I had to get new lights."

Looking at the two cars, it was amazing that these two old GM cars were so similar in style, but were in fact separated by four years and a world war. There was not a lot of automotive design progress made in Detroit while we were fighting in Europe and the Far East.

Cheryl said they also have a 1947 Chevy panel truck, which is getting finished.

"My husband got sick and can't work on the truck, so we're having someone else work on it," she said. "It's almost finished."

Might these two cars be for sale?

"We haven't really discussed it," she said.

Before we left, Cheryl gave us instructions to a road where more old cars could be found.

BAD DOG!

Car Count **4** | For Sale? YES NO MAYBE

A few miles down the road from Cheryl's on Highway 28 South we passed a used car lot with a few old relics on display. Of course we had to stop. The name of the dealership was Jackson Auto, and we were quickly greeted by Sherry Mondshour and her son, Phillip Studli. Sherry said we could look around, but her husband, James Jackson, would have to answer our questions, and he was not there at the moment.

"Don't worry about the guard dog," she said. "I'm here, so he won't bite."

So I walked to look behind the fence and... OUCH! That darn dog bit me!

James Jackson occasionally sells special-interest cars at his used car lot, including this odd but functional Plymouth coupe, which sits on a later-model chassis. It sold for $2,500.

Jackson Auto Sales also had a '64 Impala, a 1961 Desoto, and this solid-looking Falcon Ranchero.

From the rougher-than-we'd like department, this Falcon has rebuilt brakes and engine but more than its share of rust.

"Oh, I'm sorry, "said Sherry. "But don't worry, he has all his shots."

Thankfully, his teeth did not pierce my blue jeans, but his teeth clamped down hard on my kneecap, which I thought he ripped off. It left quite a dent in my skin, and I was initially worried that my running days might be over, but the pain subsided over the next few days. I was limping for a while, though.

When I called James after our trip, he said he enjoyed selling old cars.

"I don't sell many of them, but I like them," said James.

I asked about an old Plymouth that was for sale at his dealership. It was an odd combination of modern and vintage parts.

"I just sold that for $2,500. I still have a couple, though: a '61 Desoto and a '70 Chevelle."

Then our cell phone signal went dead. Not surprising since he was driving through the rural West Virginia mountains.

We left Jackson Auto and continued driving on roads that went back and forth between Maryland and West Virginia. As we entered a town called Keyser in West Virginia, we came across a couple of old cars in a yard adjacent to a body shop: an early Falcon and a first-generation Bronco.

PRETTY ROUGH

Car Count	For Sale?
2	YES NO MAYBE

These two cars were rougher than I would normally like, but they were old and we were writing a book about finding old cars, so…

They were owned by Rob Haines, owner of Rob's Body Shop, which was across the street.

"The Falcon is a 1960, the first year, I believe," Rob said. "I've had it 15 years, and my uncle had it 10 years before that.

"I started to fix it, but there's never enough money to spend on your own stuff, so it just sits. But it's new from the wheel cylinders up; rebuilt motor, new brakes. It has the 140-cubic-inch engine and vacuum wipers. It did run good, but that was a while ago."

He's owned the Bronco for 10 or 12 years.

"It's a 1969 or a '70, I think. I actually sold the Bronco. I'm taking monthly payments from an old boy. He owes me about six more months of payments before it's his."

Rob said he probably won't sell the Falcon.

"I've got to go pick up a 1964½ Mustang this week," he said. "It was also my uncle's, and he gave it to his stepson, then when he passed away, his wife gave it to me. It's been up on jacks inside the garage for 15 years, so it's in a lot better shape than the Falcon."

Parked near the Falcon at Rob's Body Shop is this rough Bronco. Owner Rob Haines said he was taking monthly payments toward its sale.

Next door to Rob's Body Shop was a mechanical repair shop called Craig Boddy Automotive. The owner, Craig, came over to see the Woody, so we started to talk. He told us there was a man up in the hills on Dry Creek Road named David Shoemaker.

"He and his wife Shirley are the nicest people you'll ever meet," said Craig. "He can repair anything, and he has a bunch of cars."

We thanked Craig and took off to find Dry Creek Road. Interestingly, our GPS told us that Dry Creek Road was right off Fried Meat Ridge Road. Hmmm. I bet they don't have any Fried Meat Ridge Roads in Miami or Beverly Hills.

FLUSH WITH CARS AT DRY CREEK ROAD

Car Count	For Sale?		
26+	YES	NO	MAYBE

We pulled up to a house that could only be David and Shirley Shoemaker's. There were old cars in the front yard, in the side yards, in buildings, and even on the roof! I knocked on the door, and the dogs started barking. Shirley Shoemaker answered the door and said her husband was working on a bulldozer on top of the hill behind their house.

"You can look around, though," she said.

So Brian, Michael, and I scattered around the yard to see what Mr. Shoemaker owned. We decided that this place was so good we would have to come back later, or even the next day, to meet and interview David in person. But within just a few minutes, David came driving up.

"I heard the dogs barking, so figured somebody was visiting," he said.

We introduced ourselves and told him we were writing a book about finding old cars and wanted to include his collection.

One of the most memorable finds during our trip came from a lead that led us to David Shoemaker's house. Wow! This 1939 Chevy is being built with period speed equipment like dual carbs, split exhaust, and a four-speed.

"Go ahead," he said.

So Michael got serious with his camera while Brian and I walked around with David from one end of his yard to the other.

"I moved in here in 1958 and got married in 1962," said David. "I never really collected cars; I've been working on them, but I sure do wish I had collected some of the ones I got rid of. I restore them for people, and some of my own. Right now I'm restoring a 1931 Model A coupe."

He showed us a 1942 Ford Business Coupe, a rare car that he bought not because it was the last model built before World War II, but because it was the year he was born. Next he showed us a 1931 Model A with a 392 Hemi with a push-button automatic and a Pinto front end.

"I was building that little hot rod for myself," he said.

In his basement garage he had a 1939 Chevy sedan that he was building into a nostalgic hot rod. It had dual carburetors and factory split exhaust.

"The engine is a 1964 231-cubic-inch six-cylinder with a cam like the Corvette had when it came out in '53," he said. "I installed an 11-inch clutch with a four-speed. I've had that quite a while, but it's been on the back burner for quite a while, too."

David's dog, Top Gun, was very protective of his master and his belongings. He went after both Michael and Brian in a good natured but aggressive way. No bites, though.

David likes both Chevys and Fords but said he is probably more of a Chevy guy.

"It's because when I first started working on cars, all parts on the 1955, '56, and '57 Chevys were interchangeable," said David. "For the '65 Mustang, hell, there were eight different brake wheel cylinders, but every Chevy part swapped onto every other Chevy."

I asked David if he had a favorite car.

David Shoemaker was one of the friendliest and most interesting people we met on the trip. He is one of the dwindling breed of Americans who can fix or build anything. I hope to visit him again one day.

One of three Tri-Five Chevys in David's garage, this is a 1955 Chevy two-door sedan.

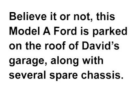

Believe it or not, this Model A Ford is parked on the roof of David's garage, along with several spare chassis.

My favorite of David's cars was this 1941 Chrysler three-window coupe. He said that President Roosevelt owned two like it! I suggested that he install one of the Hemis he had in his garage.

"Not really," he said. "I just like old cars. When these cars were built, the manufacturers took an interest in the cars they were building. Cars these days are all top dollar stuff."

He did admit that he was probably a hot rodder. I asked him this because he had engine swaps going on in virtually all his projects.

"No, well, yes, I've had a few hot rods. I still have my Henry J with a Chevy engine in it," he said.

He said he has dragged cars home from all over the South: South Carolina, Florida, Georgia, and Tennessee. He has friends who call him when they discover a car David might be interested in.

"I enjoy working on them, but my health is not the same," he said. "My legs, you know?"

David brags about the fact that he taught his daughter how to work on cars, which was later confirmed by Craig Boddy back in town. "His daughter knows how to rebuild an automatic transmission better than anyone," said Craig.

We looked at an interesting Chrysler three-window coupe.

"It's a 1941," said David. "President Roosevelt owned two just like this one. The serial number ahead of this and the one behind it are sitting in a museum. I've had this one for five or six years."

I mentioned that one of his spare Hemis would be sweet in that car, and David agreed. He also mentioned that he would probably sell the car.

"I don't have so many cars now; I used to have a bunch of them," he said. "But the state came in about 20 years ago and made me get rid of a bunch of cars. They didn't want them outside, so we had to put them everyplace we could. I got rid of a bunch of them: Fords, Chevrolets, a Cadillac. You can't believe the cars I had to crush when the state came down on me. People were actually driving old cars to the scrap yard to be crushed."

Another garage sheltered a hot-rodded 1951 Mercury four-door on the left, and a postwar Dodge coupe on the right.

David Shoemaker was one of the most interesting people I've ever met. He's talented, hardworking and humble. He reminds me of two other people: my old race car mechanic, Billy Coates; and California customizer Dean Jeffries. All three of these guys were home-taught engineers, who could fix anything.

Another "Shoebox" Ford, this one a 1949 four-door sedan. The fenders stored on the roof are from a 1941 Ford, of which David has at least one.

David had cars hidden in every corner. Here is a long-stagnant project: a 1951 Ford two-door.

I'm thankful there are still guys like David Shoemaker around; he's certainly part of a disappearing American landscape. I could have stayed on Dry Creek Road for a week talking with David, but I had a book to write, so we had to keep moving.

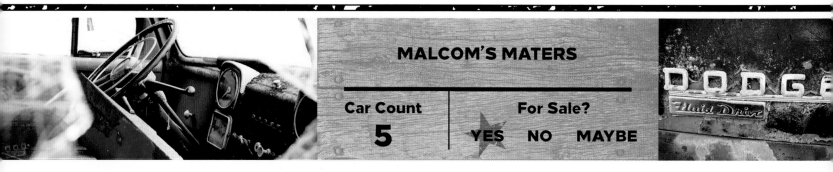

MALCOM'S MATERS

Car Count		For Sale?		
5		**YES**	**NO**	**MAYBE**

A few miles up the road, behind an auction company building, was a row of old Dodge Trucks, similar to the Mater character in the Pixar movie, *Cars.* Of course, we stopped. We met the boss of the auction business, Tim Malcolm, who told us all four trucks, 1951 through 1953, came from the same gentleman.

"He had one, and bought three more as parts trucks to restore his '52 five-window," said Tim. "I bought all four of them, but didn't pay a lot of

A few miles after leaving David Shoemaker's, we stumbled across this quartet of Dodge pickups behind an auction company. Yes, they were all for sale. Cheap.

Next to the Dodge trucks was this 1949 Oldsmobile fastback coupe, equipped with the famous Rocket 88 V-8 engine.

money for them. I'll take $3,500 for all four. They all have engines in them, but none of them turn over at the moment."

I also asked about the 1949 Oldsmobile coupe that was sitting next to the trucks.

"It comes from Romney, West Virginia, just right up the road," he said. "The owner passed away and was working on a Model A when he died. He also had a panel van, which I wanted. It was supposed to be rust-free, but it wasn't. The Oldsmobile was the most solid car he had, so I bought it."

The Olds had one of the famous Rocket V-8 engines. He said he would take $2,500 for it.

THE KEYSER

Car Count	For Sale?		
1	YES	NO	MAYBE

On Highway 220 in Keyser, West Virginia, we saw an interesting Corvair truck parked in a front yard with a For Sale sign in the windshield. Corvairs have always been interesting and curious to me, but lately I've really become intrigued with the brand. If you think about it, General Motors took a very bold step in marketing that car. In some ways, it was more Porsche than Chevrolet.

Anyway, this Corvair truck was last registered in 1980. It featured a standard three-speed transmission, AM radio, and no side-loading ramp. (Do you remember the TV ads where they featured a baby elephant walking up the ramp?) Mileage was 93,000.

Right in the middle of Keyser, West Virginia, was this Corvair pickup sitting on a front lawn with a For Sale sign on it. Off the road for 35 years, asking price for the fairly solid truck was $5,000.

This was too good to pass up as a photo op.

The woman at the house said her husband was selling the truck for a friend. The asking price was $5,000. I think the price was fair; the condition was fair as well. A restorer could do worse than fix up this truck. And you'd likely be the only Corvair pickup at your local Cars & Coffee event on any given Saturday.

It was another heck of a car-hunting day. Our plan was to drive north to Hagerstown, Maryland, for the evening, but heavy rain was forecast, so we opted for a closer hotel in Winchester, Virginia.

Virginia. Remember Virginia? We just couldn't get away from that state!

We stayed at the Aloft Hotel at exit 313, which was a nice change from our Hampton Inn ritual. Tomorrow we would cross the Mason-Dixon Line, then continue from Maryland into Pennsylvania.

We parked the Woody under the entrance portico, out of the rain, and drove the Ford Flex to dinner. We ate at the Cork Street Tavern in Winchester. I first visited the Tavern when I was racing my Morris Minor at nearby Summit Point Raceway. Now, almost 20 years later, it's still a cool place to spend an evening.

We spotted this 1949-ish Chevy delivery on the side of the road, but there was no For Sale sign, nor was anyone nearby.

DAY

Having stayed in Winchester, Virginia, we were just a few miles from one of the most respected restoration shops in the world, White Post Restorations. It was Saturday, and they would probably be closed, but we figured it would be cool to check out their facility anyway.

— ROYAL MOPARS —

We parked the Woody in the parking lot and walked around looking in windows at old cars undergoing restoration. As we were poking around, a pickup truck came pulling up and a guy in a camo outfit got out. Oh, shit, I bet we're in trouble now…

"Hi, I'm Billy Thompson," he said. "I own this place."

Obviously our 1939 Ford, which was parked prominently out front, proved that we were not up to no good.

We told Billy of our 14-day journey. He asked if we wanted to take a tour. As we walked into the building, he told us he had been out bow hunting. The season had opened this morning, and he was just getting out of the woods.

Billy runs a pretty amazing operation; all mechanical, machine, upholstery, fabrication, woodworking, and paint is handled on site. The only service they need to farm out is plating. White Post will work on any type of car or truck, from a brass-era classic to a later-model muscle car. Billy said his staff would get bored if they worked on the same type of cars all the time.

The cars we were most amazed with were five 1955 and 1956 Chrysler Imperial Limousines that were being restored for the royal family in Kuwait, who bought them new. These cars were being restored to better-than-new condition. When they arrived at White Post, they had literally been dragged from the desert where they had been riddled with bullet holes from the first Persian Gulf War.

(top) One of the Chrysler Imperial limos is nearly complete. The car, one of five, will soon be heading home to Kuwait.

(left) We stayed in Winchester, Virginia, on Friday night, so we decided to visit the world famous White Post Restorations, which was nearby. The shop was closed, but owner Billy Thompson happened along and gave us a tour.

This is one of the nine Chrysler Imperial limos required to restore the Kuwait cars.

These huge limos, weighing 6,000-pounds each and powered by Chrysler Hemi 392-cubic-inch engines, were being finished to the highest standards. The only upgrades being performed were dual air conditioning units—one for the front passenger compartment and one for the rear—instead of just the single unit that came from the factory. The cars were also being thoroughly insulated, because they would soon be shipped back to the Middle Eastern nation. Billy said they couldn't have restored the cars without acquiring a total of nine limo parts cars, which must have been quite a challenge.

That cars from a country still in military conflict were shipped to this shop in rural Virginia for restoration should give you an idea of just how well respected White Post Restorations is.

Leaving Winchester and driving north, we came across an interesting business in Berryville, Virginia. It was called Trip's Auto & Camper Sales, and, as we passed, I noticed some unusually shaped cars sitting behind the building.

We met the son of the founder, C. T. Hardesty IV, who said we could walk around and look at the old cars.

THE KUDZU TAKEBACK

Car Count
9

For Sale?
YES NO MAYBE

"My father goes by the name Trip, he's the third, and my son, Chase, is the fifth," said C. T. "Our names are all the same, Charles Triplet Hardesty. The original C. T. Hardesty was born in 1873. My dad is 84, and he's here every day. I know he'd love to talk to you."

I was immediately drawn to the 1936 Desoto Airflow sedan—AN AIRFLOW!—that was being absorbed by weeds and trees.

"I drove that car with four guys in it, parked it there in 1974, and it hasn't moved since," he said.

Wow, Airflows are quite rare. I haven't found one since about 1970, when I found one sitting in a barn on Prudence Island, off the coast of Rhode Island. The art deco styling on these cars, even though a failure in the marketplace, is fabulous to behold.

By then, Trip, his father, had arrived. Trip told us a little of the back story on the Desoto.

"I'd been an Airflow nut for years," said Trip.

Many years ago, he said he once bid on one at an auction. His limit was $800, and for $820 he could have owned it.

"I told the auctioneer, no, that's it, I've reached my limit," he said. "At that time, I really didn't have the money. Now in hindsight, I wish I had paid the other $20. That Desoto drove to where it is sitting right now. I'm getting a lot of interest in it all of a sudden, but, of course, most people who are interested want to buy it for $500.

"I bought it in Norfolk. A police officer owned it and had it advertised. When I got there, there was a fence around the car. I said to him, 'I called you and said I was on my way. Why isn't the fence down?' The seller told me he wanted to meet me first. He said if I was some kind of kid who wanted to make a street rod out of it, he wouldn't sell it to me."

Trip was not very proud of the condition he had let the Desoto deteriorate to.

"I've let many, many cars go to pot," he said. "I have a 1939 International truck back there in the field with 15,000 miles on it. I bought it at an antique car auction in 1974. I've got a 1938 Nash Ambassador with 19,000 miles on it at my son's house. It came out of the Cord, Auburn, and Duesenberg Museum and sold at the Kruse Auction."

C. T. showed us their garage, where he is restoring a 1961 Ford Starliner with a 390, and where his father's 1940 Chevy was being stored.

Just one of the many cars behind C. T. Hardesty's Camper Sales in Berryville, Virginia. This Desoto sedan is being reclaimed by nature.

The diamond in the rough at C. T.'s was this 1936 Desoto sedan, which ran when it was parked here in 1974. The race car is now a shed for hubcaps.

No, Brian, you can't steal any hubcaps!

A couple of early Ford flathead V-8 trucks being swallowed up by kudzu.

"I was driving around one night in my Starliner, and a friend came up to me and said, 'C. T., I have a car that looks like that back in my field. Only problem is that it's been converted to a saw mill.' So we jumped in his truck and drove back there in the field, and there was a 1961 Country Squire wagon, cut in half and on the back of the transmission was a big old pulley that would turn a belt. I could see under the hood that the engine had a Thunderbird logo on it, so I knew it was a big 390 motor. So I took the 352 out of my Starliner and installed the 390 from the sawmill. Except I installed a little bit different cam."

But back to the barn-find cars.

The property was littered with Buick Reattas, the semi-stylish two-seater coupes and convertibles that GM marketed for a couple of years. C. T.'s father owns 14 of them.

"*Hemming's Motor News* named the Reatta as a one of the possible top-ten collector cars of the future," said C. T. "They came with V-6 engines and front-wheel drive. When my father read that, he started buying them up."

Future barn finds? Maybe. We won't count the Reattas in our tally today, though. Sorry.

Some of the other old vehicles around the property?

"We've got my father's old farm truck over there," said Trip. "It's a 1947 [Dodge], and it has been in the family since new. Then there's a 1950 Buick fastback. It's a beauty and it was driven many years ago to where it is parked today, too. I bought it back in the mid-1970s. It is a complete car with low mileage. If it didn't have broken windows, it wouldn't be a bad car today. There are a couple of old trucks over there that I don't know much about. Then there is a GMC cabover just like the one on *Counts Customs*.

"I'm 84, and, at my age, I'm not going to worry about fixing these cars up."

Even owner C. T. Hardesty says this is a shame. This low-mileage 1950 Buick fastback sedan was driven to its location and parked. Who knows how long the windows have been broken.

Trip had been quite an entrepreneur; at one time he owned a slaughterhouse, the camper sales and service business, the used car lot, the local Department of Motor Vehicles, and a body shop. Spending time with the Hardesty family was a terrific way to waste away a Saturday morning. We said goodbye to three generations of Hardestys and continued up the road toward Fredrick, Maryland.

Granted it was a Saturday, and just about every auto-related business was closed, but the town of Fredrick didn't do anything for me. After a lifetime of searching for old cars, I've developed a feeling for an area and the ability to discover cars there. Fredrick just wasn't doing it for me.

We drove around and around, and eventually wound up in a commercial area populated with lots of truck terminals and body shops. We were waiting at a red light when I looked in my rear-view mirror and saw two guys on the sidewalk who were obviously quite interested in the Woody.

Well, we hadn't discovered anything in a while, and the day was winding down, so I put the car in reverse, cut the wheel hard to the right and pulled up next to them.

One of the guys was Dale Grimm, who owned a truck repair and towing business. The other gentleman was his employee, and they enjoyed looking at the Woody sitting at the traffic light. Dale was a hot rodder at heart and invited us into his building to see his project.

Three generations of Hardestys.

SUBURBAN POWERWAGON

Car Count	For Sale?
1	YES NO MAYBE

He was restoring a nostalgic 1931 Chevy drag car that was once famous among area racers, but it had since burned up. But the vehicle that got our attention was an unusual military truck he had in the yard.

"My son and I were riding four-wheelers in a town near here called Adamstown," said Dale. "We came across a spot where there were a bunch of old trucks: 1950s Chevrolets, 1940s Fords, a 1940-something International crane truck.

Dale Grimm of Fredrick, Maryland, found this Chevrolet PowerWagon (!) when riding four wheelers with his son. He has it mounted on a Suburban chassis.

Dale Grimm's friend George Schroyer's crowded garage contained cars like this 1957 Pontiac Chieftan, which he will either sell or customize. If the latter, he'll install a Cadillac engine.

"I've always been a Chevrolet guy, so when I saw this I thought it was a Dodge Powerwagon. But then I saw the Chevy logo on it. It's a 1941. I have the title and everything. This was originally a one-and-a-half ton, six-wheel, two-wheel drive.

"Each manufacturer, Ford, Chevy, and Dodge, had to build so many vehicles to do business with the military. They all had to have interchangeable wheels and a lot of the running gear had to be the same."

It was a complete truck when Dale bought it, but he sold the chassis to a guy who was restoring one like it.

"My son and I set the body on a Suburban chassis with a small-block in it," he said. He is considering the next step. "I'm a guy who finishes everything. I'm thinking of painting it black. I'd like to put an antique tow-truck bed on it."

Dale said he had a friend who had some unique cars outside of town.

"Follow me," he said.

We followed Dale's pickup to his friend George Schroyer's house and shop. George obviously has too much time on his hands, because he had so many projects underway.

TOO MANY PROJECTS

Car Count	For Sale?		
6	YES	NO	MAYBE

"I do repairs, mostly paint and body work on trucks," said George as he walked us into his garage.

Inside one part of the building he had a row of dusty cars, all waiting for attention. First we looked his 1965 Oldsmobile 442.

"I've had that for quite a while, probably 15 years," he said. "It has a 330-cubic-inch in it, but I have a 455 ready to go in. It's an automatic."

Now, I've always been curious about that. I have always been under the impression that the early 442 designation meant: 4 speed, 4 barrel, 2 (dual) exhaust, but I guess I am wrong.

"It depends how you ordered it," said George.

I asked if he planned to restore it.

"I'm thinking about Pro-streeting it," he said. "I even thought about chopping the top and slamming it," he said with a laugh. George was definitely a hot rodder. Even though I think it would be a shame to cut up such an original car, several of George's completed hot rods were sitting in his other garage, and they were beautiful. So I'm sure the Olds 442 would be no different.

"I used to have a junkyard, so I had a lot of cars. That's how I found this car."

OK, the car next to the Oldsmobile was a 1953 Chevy panel.

"It's been cut down into a pickup and sits on a Suburban frame with an Olds 350 in it," he said. "I have a Manley hand-crank winch to bolt into it, so it will be a vintage tow truck. I bought it from a guy who was running a little six-cylinder in it, but, when I got it, I swapped the frame and the engine. The guy cut the back of the body off before I bought it."

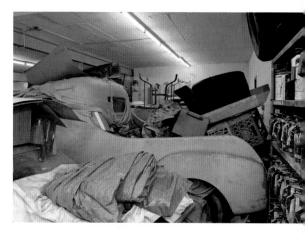

Look carefully and you'll see a '53 Chevy panel that was cut down to a pickup. It sits on a Suburban chassis and eventually will have an antique tow rig installed.

An unfinished hot rod project George owned was this fiberglass 1929 Ford roadster that was sitting in this converted truck body. He will sell it.

George dragged home this 1952 Buick rather than see it crushed at the local scrap yard. He has cannibalized parts from this Buick for other hot rod projects.

Next was a 1957 Pontiac Chieftain two-door hardtop, factory pink and black.

"The only thing I'm missing are the bumpers, that's all," said George. "It has the factory 347 engine in it with a single two-barrel. It's for sale. I have a clear title with a good body. I'll take $4,500 for it. If I keep it, I'll probably put a Cadillac motor in it, just to be different, and probably Packard taillights and extend the fenders beyond the Continental kit.

"You got to understand, I've been a hot rodder my whole life."

Before we left, George walked us out back to see a couple of cars. One was a fiberglass 1929 Ford roadster hot rod that had never been completed, which was sitting in a shed. It had a custom frame, 9-inch Ford rear, Corvair front end. And it's for sale.

And there was a Buick.

"I traded for that car," he said. "A guy who ran a junkyard called me to say he had this 1952 Buick and didn't want to crush it. So I traded another junk car for it. It was the last year for the straight-eight engine, the last year before the V-8."

"I kept it for the running gear. Four-doors don't have much demand, but I've already taken a lot of parts off it."

We said goodbye to George and followed Dale to one more old car.

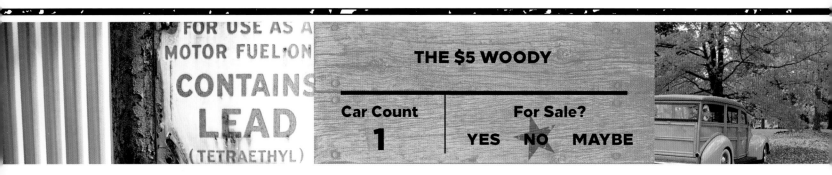

THE $5 WOODY

Car Count	For Sale?		
1	YES	NO	MAYBE

We visited one more guy, who happened to own a 1939 Ford Deluxe Woody like the one I was driving! But he purchased his in 1953 for $5! It had a rough wood body when he purchased it, so he fabricated a new one out of oak, working on it in his mother's basement after work and on weekends.

He asked that we not mention his name or give his address. Too bad, because he had a neat story to tell.

That was it for our day. We checked into a hotel in Hagerstown, Maryland, and spent 30 or 40 minutes driving around looking for a cool downtown pub, as we did every other night. However, after spending 45 minutes cruising around Hagerstown, we discovered there was no cool downtown pub. Now, wouldn't you think that a town named Hagerstown would have a historic district? Well, it did, but not much of one. And the pub there didn't appeal to the three of us, so we just went to the Mexican Restaurant across the street from the Hampton Inn.

There was a funny scene going on in there, because at the next table there were about a dozen women celebrating a bachelorette party for one of them (probably the one wearing the veil). Anyway, I suppose she was getting married in the morning, and they were pretty heavily into their Margaritas by the time we walked in. They made a lot of noise and started dancing around the restaurant to the delight of all the patrons.

They had been drinking their Margaritas through "obscene" straws, as I suppose would be appropriate for a bachelorette party. So when they got ready to leave, and were collecting all the presents and other paraphernalia, one girl yelled, "Does everyone have their penises?"

The whole restaurant erupted in laughter. It was a fun way to end the evening.

At the end of the day, Dale Grimm brought us to his friend's house. Inside the garage was this disassembled 1939 Ford Woody wagon, which was originally purchased for $5.

DAY

10

*A*nother Sunday. We certainly lucked out last Sunday when A. C. Wilson gave us a grand tour of his Buick and Cadillac collection, but I was not optimistic that we'd have the same opportunity today. My best guess was that we would drive around the countryside, enjoy the scenery, and probably start knocking on doors in the afternoon.

Wrong, Buckaroo.

We finished up our standard Hampton Inn breakfast and hit the road heading east. It was still early, about 8:30 a.m., and Brian and I were not yet on the lookout for old cars; our x-ray vision and supreme intellect had not been turned on. But driving down the road, out of the corner of my eye, I saw what appeared to be a junkyard on the right.

Couldn't be.

"I think that junkyard was open," I said to Brian. "It's early Sunday morning. Whoever heard of a junkyard open on a Sunday?"

Just to make sure, we made another one of our famous U-turns to check out what I thought I saw. It was probably just wishful thinking. But son-of-a-gun, we pulled into Elwood's Auto Exchange in Smithburg, Maryland, and the gates were wide open. Men were working. Tractors were hauling around cars.

Could this be? I walked up to a guy who looked to be in charge.

"Excuse me," I said. "Are you open?"

"Yes," said Chris Crites, the manager. "We're open every day except Christmas."

(top) Displayed like the Statue of Liberty at the entrance of Elwood's, this 1965 Ford Galaxie looked solid.

(left) Parked near the entrance of Elwood's Auto Exchange in Smithsburg, Maryland, was this 1930-ish Chevy chassis, drivetrain, and cowl. This made us optimistic about what the yard held.

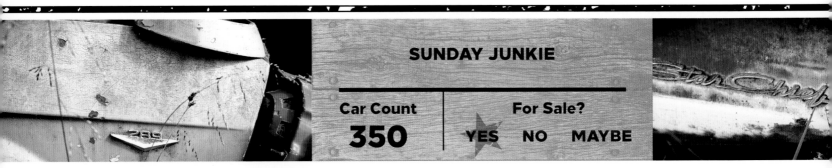

SUNDAY JUNKIE

Car Count	For Sale?
350	YES NO MAYBE

Restoration, race car, hot rod, or just parts, this V-8 Mustang held some promise that it could still live another life.

And there was the sign posted on the building:

Elwood's Auto Exchange

Smithburg, Md

Open 7 days/week

Closed Christmas

Chris said we could look around all we wanted.

"Our old stock is all in the back right corner," he said.

We parked the Woody and the Flex off to the side of the entrance, trying to keep a safe distance from trucks and tractors that were pulling cars in and out. Next to the front entrance, up on an old tractor-trailer body, a complete 1965 Ford Galaxie nose stood sentry. It looked like a yard sculpture next to all the late-model sheet metal. And it told us this yard had heritage.

Michael grabbed his camera and the three of us took off for the right rear corner of the yard. As we walked the large yard, 65 acres, we noticed that it was neatly arranged in sections by car brands; Fords in one area, Chevys in another, Mercedes-Benzes in another, and so on.

We could tell this was an old junkyard, because most of the older inventory was now parked in a thick forest, trees and bushes grown over, under, around, and through the old cars. I asked the manager when it opened, and he said 1952.

Believe it or not, collectors are beginning to restore and collect the long ridiculed Fiat 850 Spider. The cars also hold their own in vintage sports car races.

There were hundreds of old cars parked back there; we estimated 350 cars just in the right back corner. And they were mostly separated by brands: Ramblers, Fords, Mopars, Corvairs, Nashes, etc. And even though we saw the remains of a few Model Ts and Model As, most of the cars were from the 1940s into the 1960s.

In all honesty, most were pretty badly deteriorated. In my opinion, there was some street rod material, but most of the cars were ideal for parts. The cars still had valuable trim and brightwork, and most of the mechanicals were still in place.

Brian, Michael, and I felt like kids being turned loose at Disneyworld. Or Wally World. We had a good time exploring the far reaches of Elwood's, probably walking into areas that hadn't been visited in years, because their late-model junk car inventory was certainly in higher demand.

After a couple of hours, we climbed back into our vehicles and headed down the road, proud of our accomplishment of finding another stash of old cars on yet another Sunday morning.

We realized that we were probably not going to find another large stash like that this morning, but finding 350 cars before noon on a Sunday is worthy of note. It would be our single-largest find, and if we didn't find another car today, our quota was met.

So for fun we started to follow signs to an antique engine show, which turned out to be many miles off the main road, and nestled in the beautiful, rural Maryland countryside.

We had a great time walking among the "hit-and miss" engines chugging away, vintage generators, and restored lawn mowers and tractors. One guy even had a Crossley drivetrain on a stand that was running just as sweet as could be.

We decided to stay for lunch, and these folks provided a great one: pit pork barbecue sandwiches, baked beans, and lemonade. And we polished it off with a great piece of homemade pie. This was a great couple-of-hour diversion before we got back on the road.

I *think* it's a Buick, but I'm not quite sure. The right rear corner of Elwood's had dozens of cars of this era, and in this condition. Worth saving? Maybe not, but they are still out there.

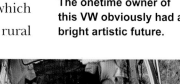

The onetime owner of this VW obviously had a bright artistic future.

This Willys was one of the few cars that could be photographed at Elwood's. Most cars were hidden among the trees and bushes that had grown around them since they were parked.

Leaving Elwood's, we were pleased to see signs for an Antique Engine Show that Sunday morning. There, we had our fill of hit-or-miss steam engines…and pie!

Since we were in Maryland, I called my friend Chuck Goldsborough, who lives in Baltimore. Chuck is a Porsche collector, and some of his barn finds have been featured in my previous *In the Barn* series of books and in *50 Shades of Rust*.

I asked Chuck if he knew of any interesting old cars in his neck of the woods. He thought for a while, then mentioned a barn full of old Porsche 356s he had heard about that had been sitting for so long that they had sunken in the dirt floor up to their axles.

"Perfect," I said. "Maybe a photo of that could be the cover of the book! Or at the very least, a stash of foreign cars would be a nice balance to the large amount of domestic cars we were discovering."

Chuck told me he would make some phone calls and get back with me. Another call from Chuck, and he told me where we could meet him. Obviously he knows my sweet spot.

"I couldn't track down the Porsche guy, so we'll meet me at Baugher's Restaurant in Westminster [Maryland]," he said. "We'll have some of their great homemade ice cream and then go over to my friend John's house to see his Corvettes."

Great! But before we met Chuck at the ice cream stand, the Woody started to give us trouble again.

Remember our Woody broke down a couple of days earlier when the air conditioning compressor failed? Well, we installed a shorter serpentine belt that eliminated the a/c compressor and everything was fine. Or so we thought…

Apparently we should have chosen an even shorter belt, because the bottom of the alternator had been rubbing against a high-pressure steel line coming off the rack and pinion steering unit. A hole wore through the line and all the power steering fluid had escaped.

John Grata's yard and buildings had too many interesting cars! This MGB GT, sitting in the weeds, was reputedly built by race car wizard Smokey Yunick.

Suddenly steering was much tougher. I called my friend Keith Irwin in Concord, North Carolina, and he told me if I drove a long distance without fluid in the steering system, I could potentially seize the power steering pump and damage the steering rack.

We needed to find a replacement steel line. So when Chuck pulled into the parking lot at the ice cream stand, I broke the news to him that the Woody was kaput. Chuck had a solution. "My brother owns a service station," he said. "You can bring it over there and we'll put it on the lift."

Poifect!

But in the meantime, we had a bunch of Corvettes to look at. Chuck suggested we leave the Woody in Baugher's parking lot, visit his friend John, then come back later to pick up the Woody and drive it to his brother's garage.

I jumped into Chuck's monster 4X4 Dodge truck (with HUGE air horns that almost knocked me off my feet; I'll get you back, Goldsborough, you bastard!), with Michael and Brian following in the Flex. We drove several miles and then turned down a long dirt driveway. I guess John lived back in the woods.

Suddenly we entered a pastoral setting scattered with a bunch of buildings. We pulled up to the largest building and a guy came out to meet us. Chuck introduced us to John Grata, who services, restores, and collects Corvettes. His specialty is early fuel-injected cars. He also owns an antique mall in Pennsylvania. And, interestingly, when he was a teenager, Chuck used to work for John after school.

TOO MANY VETTES

Car Count	For Sale?		
60	YES	NO	MAYBE

This 1957 Chevy two-door wagon was an unfinished project. It sat protected under a shed roof and seemed solid.

We walked around with John, looking at some of the vehicles scattered around his property. Here was a 1957 Chevy two-door wagon; it was a decent car John said he bought seven or eight years ago at auction. And there were a couple of 1930s Ford pickup cabs he bought a day ago at the Carlisle flea market; he needs them to repair a third truck he is building. His collection was large and eclectic.

He said he's been in this location since 1978. And he said he has acquired too many projects.

"I want to restore six or eight cars to drive," he said. "The rest just need to go away. I just don't have the time to work on all of them. I have a deal on two cars inside, and they'll go away next week."

John specializes in rebuilding Rochester Fuel Injection units for 1950s and 1960s Corvettes. He said that alone keeps him too busy. And he builds engines.

I asked about a Corvette that was sitting in the weeds.

"I worked on that car 20 years ago," he said. "It belonged to a dentist. And the guy turned into a drug addict and never came back to get it. I don't think he's even alive anymore. It's a 1976 and it has the high horsepower engine and a four-speed." It had been sitting there so long that much of the paint on the hood, trunk, and roof was flaking off, exposing the raw fiberglass.

What a shame; a drug-addict dentist left this '76 Corvette at John's for repair work 20 years ago and never returned to pick it up.

We walked up to an early car, also in the weeds.

"That was the first Corvette I ever bought," he said. "It's a 1962, and I bought it without an engine. I put a built-up 327 in it, and it would pull the front wheels off the ground."

Then there was a 1958 Corvette, which happens to be my personal favorite early-model Corvette. I really dig the faux hood vents and the two chrome strips on the trunk.

"It's a fuelie car," said John. "I bought it just like this. And there's another '58 fuelie car. I bought it about four months ago."

Man, this guy has the Vettes.

But John is not totally a Corvette guy. There, parked next to his building, was a 1940 Ford panel truck. In what must be the oddest engine transplant of all time, the truck had a Ford 300-cubic-inch straight-six-cylinder engine—probably 1960s vintage—with a four-barrel carburetor.

"It has an Offenshauser intake manifold and a C-4 automatic transmission," he said. "And it has a Deluxe passenger car nose, instead of the commercial nose. I have gathered all the parts to put this back together, and bought a second truck as well."

This '62 Corvette sits inside another shed. John has been into Corvettes for 40 years. He's bought them for as little as $800.

John has owned many of his Corvettes for decades, but this 1958 fuel-injected model was purchased just a few months before we saw it.

One of the oddest vehicles in John's eclectic inventory was this 1940 Ford panel delivery, which had a Deluxe passenger car grill and a Ford straight-six-cylinder engine.

Finally we got inside John's building, where the real gems were hiding. This coupe had a fresh paint job when restoration was halted.

Sounds like the typical car guy; he doesn't need the first truck, so he bought a second one. He did tell me these trucks are for sale.

We were now inside his building, which was large and cluttered. John pointed out a '64 Stingray that had belonged to a friend of his.

"It got crashed about 10 years ago. The owner loaned it to someone, and this guy pulled out in front of someone and the front end got knocked off. I may fix it. Time is the issue."

John said he does all his own fiberglass and paint work.

He pointed out a 1932 Ford panel truck inside the cluttered building.

"It's the old Culligan truck," John said as he pointed out the lettering on the side of the body. That's my winter project. It's going on a J&W Chassis, a built-up Ford 302 with a five-speed with air conditioning. It will be a keeper and a driver."

Some of the other cars in the building: '64 Impala SS (300 horsepower, four speed); 1955 Chevrolet Suburban (327, automatic); black 1966 Stingray coupe (a/c,

One of my personal favorites in John's collection was this 1962 fuel-injected Corvette. If I owned this car, I would clean it up and use it as-is.

John restores cars for customers and does all mechanical, bodywork, and paint in his shop. This coupe is receiving major body repair.

360 horsepower, disc brakes, original knock-off wheels and side pipes); 1957 Pontiac Safari wagon (rust-free Arizona car, Tri-Power, with a spare Smokey Yunick—built 377-cubic-inch engine); 1965 Corvette a/c car; 1957 Chevy sedan delivery (owned 25 years); a 1966 Pontiac GTO with four-speed; a 1968 Camaro RS/SS convertible; 1962 Corvette that he uses to test run his rebuilt fuel-injection units before sending them back to customers; 1965 Corvette coupe that John drove for a number of years; and more. John admits that he bought most of his Corvettes at the right time. For some of them he paid as little as $800.

And, until recently, John also owned a Rangoon Red 289 Cobra that he purchased about 40 years ago.

John brought us into another garage, where he had a very nice 1940 Ford Standard 60-horsepower coupe and *the last* 1966 Shelby Mustang GT350 ever built.

John said he has never advertised his cars or business, and yet he has more work than he can handle.

I think we could have spent another hour, or a week or two, with John, listening to his stories, but the

And now for something completely different. This 1957 Pontiac Safari wagon has a Tri-Power engine and is free of rust.

Something Completely Different, Part II. I never expected to see a Mustang among John's Corvette collection. This is the last 1966 Shelby GT350 built.

A broken Woody again. For some reason all the power steering fluid leaked out and made the Woody hard to drive. We needed to find a place to work on it Sunday evening.

sun was going down and we needed to pick up the Woody and see if we could repair it. So we said goodbye to John and reversed our direction on his long dirt driveway.

Back at the ice cream stand, I jumped into the Woody and followed Chuck in the very fast Dodge truck. Driving the Woody without power steering was tough, but not impossible. We drove to Chuck's brother's repair shop in Baltimore and put the car up on the lift.

"Oh, we just need to have a new high-pressure line fabricated," I said. "We'll take that line off and, when a hydraulic shop opens in the morning, we'll have a new one made, and we'll be back on the road in no time."

That evening we went to Chuck's favorite Italian restaurant, La Famiglia, in historic Roland Park, Maryland. Because he was so helpful, I treated him and his brother, Emmett, to dinner. And we may have had a little too much red wine. Thankfully our hotel was just a two-block walk away.

We all had a good night's sleep and woke up early to begin looking for a shop that could fabricate that hydraulic line.

This proved to be fruitless.

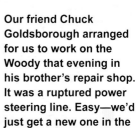

Our friend Chuck Goldsborough arranged for us to work on the Woody that evening in his brother's repair shop. It was a ruptured power steering line. Easy—we'd just get a new one in the morning. Ha!

Before fixing the Woody, we sprung for some homemade ice cream. We all have priorities. Ice cream is one of mine.

DAY

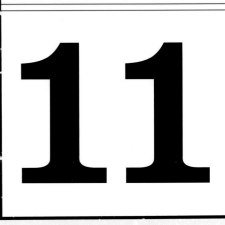

—— WOODY REPAIR II ——

We went from one hydraulic shop to another and another. Three shops, and none of them could make a line with a compression fitting like we needed. They had actually never seen a high-pressure fitting like it before.

How could this be? What will we do?

Then Brian had a brilliant idea. "What if we buy a rebuilt steering rack from an auto parts store?" he asked. "I'll bet that would have the correct line attached."

We drove to an Advance Auto, looked at a steering rack for a Mustang II, and Brian was correct!

So we bought the $60 rebuilt steering rack in order to get a steel line that was probably worth $5. But by noon we were back on the road, ready to hunt for more cars.

(By the way, if you know of anyone who needs a rebuilt power steering rack for a Mustang II, minus one steel line, let me know; I have one in my garage…)

I asked Chuck whether he had heard any more about all the Porsche 356s in the barn, but he had not heard back from the owner yet. But he did recommend another interesting collection of cars north of Baltimore that we could look at in the meantime.

So we headed to one of the most incredible automotive sights I've ever seen.

(top) Because of the Woody repair, we only made one find on Monday. But what a find! Chuck led us to a house that had the most amazing collection of cars, such as this Trabant wagon.

(left) Mike has the most eclectic collection of cars. It cannot be categorized. This '57 Chevy four-door is one of several Tri-Five Chevys he owns.

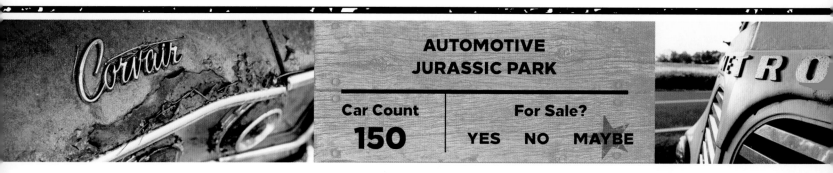

AUTOMOTIVE
JURASSIC PARK

Car Count	For Sale?		
150	YES	NO	MAYBE

We followed Chuck from highways to rural roads, until we came across a residential yard that was littered with dozens of interesting old cars: old Divco milk trucks, Corvairs, East European Trabants; all spread across the front yard.

This was amazing.

We parked our cars and walked around with our mouths gaping. I honestly don't know if I've ever seen a collection quite like this. I have an eclectic automotive taste, so to me seeing collections of only Thunderbirds or Jaguars is not half as interesting as this.

Just one of a number of Divco milk trucks that Mike owns. These have been rented for use in a number of movies.

How's this for diversity? A 1953 Cadillac sedan and a Corvair share the parking lot in the side yard.

Ready? Yugos, Chevys (1955, '57), Trabants (passenger cars, Jeep-types, and wagons), Caddys, Corvairs (sedans, vans, and pickups), VWs (Beetles and buses), Fords (domestic, English Prefects, and Zephers), a Plymouth Barracuda, an International Harvester, mid-'60s T-Bird roadster and more and more and more.

And that is just what I could see in the front and side yard and through the fence. There were many, many more cars in the backyard I could not see because it was blocked by all the bamboo! (Remember bamboo?) I had to talk to the owner. I knocked on the door and met Andrew Annen. He said his father, Mike, owned the cars, and that he was at work.

"I'll call him and see when he'll be home," said Andrew as he walked back into the house.

When he came back, he said his father would be home after 7:00 p.m., and that he'd be glad to meet us. But until then, Andrew would be glad to show us some of the cars in the front and side yards. We started out looking at the Trabants, a brand that was manufactured in Eastern Europe during the cold war. They were two-cylinder, 2-cycle, air-cooled, and front-wheel drive. And they had the reputation of being smoky and slow.

"These have metal subframes and a body made of cotton fiber," said Andrew. "They take cotton—basically old clothes—and press it with resin and it turns into a hard, almost plastic-like material."

Andrew said they can smoke badly if oil is mixed incorrectly. In reality, they are like the two-stroke engines in a Lawn Boy lawn mower.

"It's like a weed wacker," he said. "The earlier ones smoke a lot. My father has been bringing them in from out of the country." He pointed to a Trabant military vehicle, which I just could not imagine going to war with.

"My dad's been into Trabants since about 2004," he said. When I asked what type of car his father drives every day, I was surprised to find out it was a Mitsubishi

A very solid 1959 Ford two-door sedan and one of several VW buses in the side yard. And we haven't even visited the backyard yet. That will come this evening.

Michael aimed his camera over the fence and this is what he saw! Let me see—right to left, I think it's a Trabant, a Vespa, and a Model A Ford Deluxe cabriolet.

(top) The interior of this English Ford Prefect sedan is being kept out of the weather with a handy pickup truck cap.

(above) Mike gave us a tour of his backyard in the dark, which added to the intrigue. This Austin Healey Bugeye Sprite has seen better days, but it runs! In the background is another Trabant wagon.

electric car. "He had been into big American cars, but then he started to get into smaller European stuff," said Andrew. "Now Trabants are his next big adventure."

Andrew told me that Trabants are pretty reasonably priced. "Depending on their condition, about $3,000 for a running daily driver. They are EPA and DOT exempt, because they are more than 25 years old."

This was a serious find, and I was so glad Mike agreed to talk to us. I gave Andrew a copy of my *50 Shades of Rust* book, which had just been released. "Here, give this to your father," I said. "We'll be back after 7:00."

We left with Chuck for a terrific meal a few miles down the road at a place called the Manor Tavern. Great place in Monkton, Maryland, smack dab in the middle of horse country. We had some great food; I had the baby back ribs with their special homemade barbecue sauce, which had quite a kick! And there was a kicking bluegrass band playing as well. It was a neat place, and some of the patrons at the bar approached us to talk about our Woody in the parking lot.

Almost two hours later, it was getting dark and was time for us to go back to Mike's house so we could meet the man in person.

Chuck said goodbye, having spent almost two entire days with us. He needed to go back home to spend some quality time with his family. Before I said goodbye

Something you don't see every day—a rare Citroen 2 CV panel delivery truck, minus one front wheel.

to Chuck, I reminded him that I would still like to see that barn full of old Porsches while I was in the area. He promised to find out about their status and call us in the morning. With that, we headed back up the road to Mike's house.

I knocked on the door and Mike invited me inside. He had been reading the *50 Shades* book, so he had a good idea of who I was before we met. Even though it was dark out—almost 8:00 p.m. by now—he offered to take us on a tour of his backyard and buildings. He provided the flashlights. But first he wanted to check out my Woody. Mike was a real car guy.

He started to discuss the Trabants. He said his son Mathew was operating the website www.trabantusa.com and that there are close to 100 members nationwide.

"It was actually Tom Brokaw that got me into Trabants," he said. "We had been watching the news about the Berlin Wall coming down, and I became intrigued with the little cars."

Eventually Mike was bringing home shipping containers full of Trabants from Europe. He said he's paid as little as $25 for them plus $9 customs fees. He could stack six in a container. He's traveled to England, Germany, Poland, and Hungary on Trabant buying trips.

(top) **This is me standing next to a Morris Minor sedan and looking upstairs in Mike's barn. He has cars on ground level and more upstairs!**

(below) **A couple more Citroen 2 CV coupes. The spunky, two-cylinder cars have a suspension that supposedly can carry a basket of eggs across a plowed farm field without breaking any!**

Not really a "Woody," this 1951 Chevy had a metal body that was painted to look like wood. The interior, however, contains real wood.

(above) **This Porsche 914 doesn't look like it's been driven in a long, long time. Don't get excited; it's not a six-cylinder.**

(above right) **Brian finds another barn on Mike's property and decides to explore…**

OK, enough with the Trabants. What else did Mike have?

"My first car was a 1969 Chevelle that I wrapped up and kept on rebuilding," he said. "Then I bought another Chevelle, which was an SS 396. I still have that car in the barn.

"My first old car I found in 1978 while riding around during high school and it was a 1950 Buick Sedanette. It was a straight-eight with a Dynaflow transmission. The gas mileage sucked. Then I got into Divco milk trucks for a while. I bought a bunch and have rented them out for movies. I bought 11 for $2,200 from a laundry near DC that was closing. I made money renting them out, and when the movie was over, I sold one truck for $3,000. I still have about nine left."

Mike told me about the challenges of owning that many cars in a residential area. He must register each vehicle with Maryland Historic tags, and has to deal occasionally with police officers who decide to walk through his property to inspect license plate tags.

Other cars on Mike's property: Model T; Model A; '47 Chevy Coupe (semi hot rodded); DKW (freshly restored); '51 Chevy hardtop with Cadillac fins; Renault;

Inside he finds a small-mouth Triumph TR3 that seems to be covered in surface rust.

Oldsmobile; 1953 and 1954 Chryslers; Fiat (couple of 850s); International tow truck; 1961 Buick Skylark convertible; Citroen 2 CV; and on and on.

This 1947 Pontiac four-door sedan seems to be returning to the earth.

Most of the cars in the rear of Mike's property were buried in a bamboo forest, which hides most of the cars until you are right on top of them. Mike said that if he cuts the bamboo, it grows back quickly. He's given up on trying to keep it mowed down.

And to make this discovery even more insane, Mike has another 150 cars in a building on a piece of property he owns in West Virginia! I asked him how he planned to deplete his collection one day; would he have an auction, or sell them off one by one?

"I guess when I go, the old lady is going to have a big junk sale," he said with a big smile.

This is the first Checker we've found on the Barn Find Road Trip. Mike rents his cars and truck out to movies being shot in and around Washington D.C. This Checker taxi was in one of those movies.

One lone French Renault Dauphine sits in the dark next to another French car, a Peugeot.

To me this was the most significant find of our 14-week adventure, and one of the best finds of my life. Mike knew he had the car sickness real bad, and joked about it. He was a great guy and was so kind in allowing us to see his collection. He said that he never gives tours of his property, so we felt very lucky.

I seriously could have spent another 8 or 10 hours walking through that bamboo forest and listening to Mike's stories. This was a discovery that car geeks dream about stumbling upon once in their lives. It was a great adventure, and I hope to come back for another visit when I am in the area.

We headed off to our hotel. It had been a long, long day. Time to call it quits. I believe I could write a book just about Mike's collection. What a day.

This postwar Chevy sedan seems to be getting squeezed out by trees on both sides!

(opposite) Visiting Mike's yard caused sensory overload, especially in the evening. Before we departed, Michael (our photographer) got a little artistic with a '57 Chevy tailfin and the moon.

DAY

12

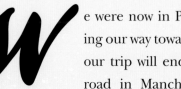e were now in Pennsylvania, making our way toward Hershey, where our trip will end. Driving down a road in Manchester, we saw an older gas station-type building on the left that had a couple of old cars sitting outside—a Camaro and a Porsche.

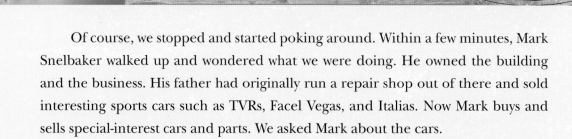

ROUGH BUT INTERESTING

Car Count	For Sale?
5	YES NO MAYBE

Of course, we stopped and started poking around. Within a few minutes, Mark Snelbaker walked up and wondered what we were doing. He owned the building and the business. His father had originally run a repair shop out of there and sold interesting sports cars such as TVRs, Facel Vegas, and Italias. Now Mark buys and sells special-interest cars and parts. We asked Mark about the cars.

"I've been messing around with cars all my life," said Mark. "I started with old Camaros. My first car was a '69 RS/SS."

I asked about the 1968 Camaro next to his building.

"It's for sale," he said. "It's a plain Camaro with an automatic on the floor. I bought it at a flea market. I have a '69 Z28 out back, code X77. That car is not for sale."

Then I asked about the Porsche, which was pretty rough.

"I bought it off a buddy of mine. It's a four-cylinder, and it's for sale. I'd sell it for $1,000 or make an offer. It's been sitting for years."

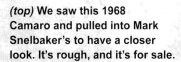

(top) We saw this 1968 Camaro and pulled into Mark Snelbaker's to have a closer look. It's rough, and it's for sale.

(left) This Porsche 914 has seen better days. Mark said he'd like to sell it for $1,000. He has a couple sets of alloy wheels for the car that are available as well.

Mark had a 1962 Vette in high school, so he couldn't turn down buying another one. But it sits ignored in his building waiting for Mark to find the time to restore it.

The other car outside was an Olds Delta 88 convertible, but with the convertible top ripped and the rain running in, I can't see why someone would want to restore that car. Mark also owns a 1962 Corvette. It was inside the building and literally buried with clutter. It's a basket-case project, and it's not for sale.

"I've had it for 20 years," he said. "When I was 18, I had a '62 Vette, but I had to sell it for financial reasons. I always said I'd get another one, so I did. Now I'd just like to drive it."

Inside his building, he has lots of interesting car parts—like grilles and taillights—that he sells on the Internet. As a result, he keeps lots of boxes around for shipping parts. And he piles those boxes on top of the Corvette.

Before we left Mark's business, he looked at our Woody and mentioned that just three houses away were a couple of brothers who restore Woodies full-time.

"What's their name?" I asked.

"Their last name is Kline," he said.

Believe it or not, this 1969 Camaro once left a Chevy dealership as a shiny, new Z-28! Mark said he hopes to find the time to make it shiny again.

WOODY WOODPECKERS

Car Count	For Sale?
1	YES NO MAYBE

I had seen their ads in the National Woodie Club's *Woodie Times* magazine.

"Well, I guess we'll go there next," I said.

I parked the Woody next to the Kline Family Workshop and walked in. I met Tom and Mike Kline, who, in fact, restore Woody wagons full-time. Tom kindly gave me a tour of his shop and gave me a Woodworking #101 course. He told me business is good.

"I don't know if it will slow down, but right now it's all I can do just to keep up," he said. "We've got plenty of work lined up."

Tom mentioned that they do mostly Ford Woody restorations, just because there are more Ford Woodies around. But he will take on any wooden car, regardless of brand. He has done a number of Plymouths, Buicks, a couple of Chevys, and a Rolls Royce that needed interior woodwork. In his shop was a 1949 Plymouth that was getting a new body installed.

Just three houses from Mark Snelbaker's shop is the Kline Family Woodworking shops, one of the most renowned wood body restorers in the country. This 1949 Plymouth was getting a new body installed.

I asked if he owned a Woody.

"I don't have one," he said. "I've got an old Dodge Powerwagon out back that we were going to make a Woody out of, but it's just sitting there. When you're doing this every day, it's no fun to do it evenings as well. I'd rather do something else."

In addition to Woody wagons, the Klines have also built new bodies for a couple of Chrysler Town & Country convertibles and sedans.

One fascinating machine Tom showed me was a wood carving machine, which allowed the user to cut a left and right side pattern at the same time. It makes a mirror image of items, like door posts, that are virtually identical from side to side. Pretty cool. Almost like a primitive CNC machine.

The Klines fabricate and install Woody bodies and also sell kits for customers to install themselves. These guys are master woodworkers. The work they do is nothing less than old world craftsmanship. I would gladly recommend Kline to perform woody restorations.

We said goodbye to Tom and Mike and wandered off to our next adventure, wherever that was...

Tom and Mike Kline bought this Dodge Powerwagon with the intention of making it into a "phantom" Woody. But the desire to work on their own car has diminished.

ANONYMOUS AUTONOMOUS MUSTANG MAN

Car Count	For Sale?
5	YES NO MAYBE

Just a block away from the Klines, we stumbled into another interesting guy who owned a bunch of restored and original Fords and Mustangs, including a 1931 Ford Model A pickup, 1966 Mustang GT convertible, 1967 Shelby GT 500, 1968 Mustang drag car, and a 1969 Mach One. We enjoyed talking with him, but he didn't want us to use his name or photos in the book, so we said goodbye and hit the road again.

— ON THE WAY TO POSIES...WHOOPS! —

We were on a path to Hershey, Pennsylvania, for the annual swap meet and car show. Before we got there, though, I wanted to stop at Posies Rods and Customs in nearby Hummelstown. But our GPS guided us to a bridge that was closed for repairs, so we kept driving up the road on the wrong side of the river from where we wanted to be while Brian and Siri argued over the directions his iPhone was giving us.

A few miles up the river, we saw an old, rusty Ford in a pasture, so we pulled in the driveway to inspect it. It was a 1937 Ford two-door sedan with a 1940 dashboard installed. And it was *so* rusty. Barely good as a parts car, if you ask me.

BOB'S BARN FINDS

Car Count	For Sale?	
6	YES NO MAYBE	

We walked up to the shop and met Bob Moyer, who was a car collector, hot rodder, vintage stock-car racer and farmer. Bob invited us into his garage to see some of his projects. Sitting next to the garage door was a 1949 Ford two-door sedan that he was in the process of building into a vintage stock car. Looked like he was doing a good job, and having a great time doing it.

Around the side under a carport was a barn-find 1951 Mercury four-door sedan that he had acquired. No restoration required; this baby was solid and a great driver.

"The gentleman bought this car new in 1951, and he died in 1960, so they put it in the barn, and I got it out in 2005. I bought it from the old man's son. He said, 'What will you give me for it?' and I said '$4,000.' The guy started to laugh. He thought it was worth $50!"

When he brought it home, he had 45 years' worth of cleaning to do.

"It was covered in pigeon shit," said Bob. "So I gave each of my three grandchildren a Brillo pad and they cleaned it. Then I hit it with compound. And the mice had the whole interior moved into the trunk!"

He also had a nice 1966 Mercury Comet with a 390-cubic-inch and a four-speed.

"I'm an old flathead guy," said Bob. He showed us a flathead-powered Modified racer that had been campaigned in the area around the time Bob was in military service.

This rusty hulk of a 1937 Ford in Bob Moyer's farm field attracted our attention. An advertising headline around this photo might read "One of These Cars Used Simonize, and the Other Didn't."

Bob dragged home this 1951 Mercury after it had sat for 45 years. A general clean-up, which included scraping years of pigeon crap from the body, made this a presentable, unrestored car.

"It was a barn find. We found it. There was an old speedway around here, which is now defunct. It was Silver Springs Speedway up in Mechanicsburg. It was one of the most popular speedways in its day. And we found this car; here's a tech inspection sticker, September 14, 1968. A photographer sent me an old picture of the car, which is the only one I have."

He recently displayed this car at the Eastern Museum of Motor Racing in York Springs, Pennsylvania. He plans on running the car on the track at next year's vintage event.

Bob told me there probably weren't too many old cars in the immediate area.

"I've lived around here my whole life and been in and out of most every barn, and I can tell you, most of the cars are accounted for."

Then Bob raised another garage door and revealed what he calls his "Old Man's car." "I take my mom to church in this car," he said as he showed us a 1959 Rambler Custom with 41,000 miles on the odometer. It was sweet.

We asked about the rusty 1937 Ford that attracted us into Bob's yard in the first place. He said it was a sad story.

"There was a junkyard on the other side of those mountains," he said. "Someone said they were going to go over to the junkyard to get something. I asked, 'What junkyard?' My friend said, 'Evan's Junkyard.' I'd never heard of it, and I'd been through every back lane around. So I drove up the dirt road and thought, 'Maybe I shouldn't be here…'

"But here was this junkyard, about 300 to 400 cars, nothing newer than 1955 or '56. My jaw was on the ground. I couldn't believe it, every car was $200. He had Model As with trees growing through them. Well, anyway, someone came along and bought just about all the cars, but I found this old '37 hiding up in the woods. So I paid $200 and got the car."

Bob's current project is this 1949 Ford sedan, which he is converting into a vintage-style stock car.

Inside the trunk of the car was a bucket with eight Stromberg Carburetors, a banjo steering wheel, and extra axles as well. "It had $1,000 worth of spare parts in the trunk alone," Bob told us. The car has been sitting in his field for the past five years.

Despite the sedan's awful condition, Bob is considering a partial restoration of the car to prove to his friend that anything can be repaired. Good luck!

This was the perfect detour; the bridge being closed en route to Posies allowed us to meet Bob, see his cars, and hear his stories.

Old cars are everywhere!

Bob dug up this vintage Modified racer, which had history racing at local tracks in this part of Pennsylvania. He hopes to race it at the Eastern Museum of Auto Racing vintage event next year.

FINALLY, ON TO POSIES

Car Count	For Sale?		
1	YES	NO	MAYBE

Posies Rods and Customs is owned by my friend Ken Fenical and is one of the top hot rod shops in the United States. Ken is a hot rodder through and through, but he is also an artist and a sculptor. The work he turns out is world class. His cars have been featured in books, magazines, and car shows throughout the United States.

To get a handle on Posies' work, check out www. posiesrodsandcustoms.com. Cars are his palette, and sheet metal is his medium. As opposed to most street rod builders who install modern drivetrains in vintage bodies, Ken can't leave well enough alone; he reshapes metal, re-contours body lines, and builds trim and emblems that are suitable for museum display. Check out the website for his *Extremeliner, Swept Back, Orange Krisp,* and Jaguar-based

We finally made it to Posies Rods and Customs in Hummelstown, Pennsylvania. Parked out in front was owner Ken Fenical's daily driver, this Chevy-powered Jaguar coupe that he named *Flat Cat*.

Ken shows me some of the projects going on in his shop.

Flat Cat. His cars very much resemble the custom coachwork from UK or Italian-based body craftsmen.

Ken is not a barn finder, so to speak. Most of his clients bring cars to him for modification. So, except for a couple of cars he knew about that were sitting in a nearby front yard, he didn't know about any huge collections of barn-find cars. But when I pressed Ken, he said, "Well, there is the old panel truck in the back."

Indeed there was.

Posies had a terrific barn find literally sitting in the back of their building, in a dark room, all but forgotten. Ken has owned the 1930 Model A for 51 years.

"I paid $350 for it, and had my choice of either a 1929 or the '30," he said. "It became my daily driver for 25 years."

He told us about pulling out the original four-cylinder using a tree branch in his father's yard. Then he towed the panel truck to a junkyard, where they lowered a Chevy V-8 into the chassis, where it rested on 2x4s. He trailered it home and welded in mounts.

"I made a Ford Econoline front axle work," he said.

The drivetrain is nothing exotic, but being his daily driver, it didn't have to be; it has a Chevy 307-cubic-inch with a Powerglide two-speed automatic. When I told

Michael, right, is always stuck on the other side of the camera, while Brian is photo-bombing every chance he gets. So I shot the photo as Michael posed with Ken.

See, there's that photo-bombing Brian, trying to look cool in front of Ken's *Flat Cat* Jag.

Ken he indeed did have a barn find, he thought maybe he would take it out of the garage and get it running again.

"I won't even clean the dust off it," he said with a smile.

And there was a lot of dust!

—— TIME FOR A BREW ——

We said goodbye to Ken and the staff at Posie's and hit the road for nearby Hershey. But we wouldn't hit the swap meet just yet. Evening was approaching, so when we got to Hershey we drove straight to Troeg's Brewery, which is just up the street from the swap meet site.

Brian and I had visited Troeg's on a previous road trip and enjoyed their craft beer and amazing food. We felt it might be a good place to not only catch dinner, but meet with other patrons who might be old-car enthusiasts in town for the big event.

Well, the food and beverage were great, as usual, but we couldn't connect with any other car people. The place was jammed and noisy, and everyone seemed to be in large groups that were hard to break into. We were staying in Carlisle, about 35 minutes south, so we decided to get on the road so we could check into the hotel, a Hampton Inn, of course. Tomorrow would be another long day.

Ken tells us the story of his very first shop truck. He paid $350 for it and pulled the original engine using a tree in his parent's front yard.

Ken did finally admit that he owned a barn find... that he found in his own warehouse! He has owned this 1930 Model A Panel since 1963.

DAY

*I*f we judged each day's success by the number of vehicles we discovered, yesterday was probably our least productive. Still, we met some cool folks and found some cool cars.

Now our plan was to spend a couple of days at the Hershey swap meet. By walking through the flea market and car corral area, we felt finding cool barn finds would be as easy as shooting fish in a barrel.

Because the three of us also spent time searching for parts for project cars, and I had a couple of book signings scheduled, I decided to count Days 13, 14, and 15 as one day. We found several pretty cool old cars at Hershey, but not as many as you might think. In no particular order, here are the barn-find "highlights" we "discovered" on the Hershey grounds over the three days we attended.

—— 1932 CHEVY PANEL DELIVERY ——

Jim Mack had known about this Chevy for a long time, but the owner did not want to sell.

"The owner had it for 50 years, and would only take it out once or twice a year, like to the Apple Festival parade," said Jim, an Ohio-based car collector. "Each year, he would give it a kerosene bath and put it away for the winter. The kerosene preserved the body and kept the moisture away."

Jim explained that the owner also had a 1931 Ford Model A roadster in that same barn. "He got married in the roadster," said Jim. "He also had a 1946 Ford convertible. I went there four years ago, but nothing was for sale. Then the family called me last May and told me their dad's health was failing."

They had sold Jim the Model A, which is Jim's specialty, and the Chevy panel truck a couple of months before Hershey. I am a serious Ford guy, but this panel truck really got my attention. The style was very Ford-like, and the condition was extremely good for a never-restored vehicle.

(top) This unrestored 1932 Chevy panel really got our attention. The truck was amazingly solid and ran well. It was being sold by Jim Mack, who usually deals in Model A Fords.

(left) When we arrived in Hershey, we parked the Woody next to the Society of Automotive Historians tent. We left some of our stickers on the windshield for people to take.

Jim told me about his method of searching for old cars.

"I go out West two or three times a year," he said. "You've got to get off the beaten path; you can't stay on I-80. But they are still out there. I was out there two or three weeks ago and attended an estate auction at a house that was built in the 1950s or '60s, in a neighborhood where you would never imagine a car collection. But at one time there had been 50 cars at this home, although there were only about 20 left at the time of the sale."

Need a fender? How about a complete body? If you've never been to Hershey, I highly recommend you plan to visit during the second week of October.

This 1927 Pierce Arrow was particularly solid—and running. Seller Greg Long of Michigan said the car only needed shocks. For less than $20,000, someone could own a running, driving classic.

— 1927 PIERCE ARROW —

Greg Long of Holly, Michigan, picked up this Pierce Arrow in Ontario, Canada, just seven days before the Hershey event.

"It has 1944 and 1952 inspection stickers on it," said Long. "The previous owner had purchased it as a parts car, but only removed the shocks. At one time it had been left over the winter with water in the engine, so the head cracked. I'm a member of the Pierce Arrow Society, and our mission is to keep the collector hobby alive."

Greg said that he bought it and got it running before bringing it to Hershey.

"Someone can be into this car for less than $20,000. It was the company's lowest priced closed car, selling for $3,500 new. For comparison, the company's roadster was $2,700. I got it in a 'Grandpa is getting old, so we're finally going to sell it,' type of deal. Pretty typical."

Interestingly Brian's grandfather worked at Pierce Arrow in Buffalo, New York, as a tool-and-die maker. His handiwork was likely involved in the manufacture of this very Pierce.

Brian posing with the Pierce Arrow, which was manufactured in Buffalo, New York. Brian's grandfather worked for the company about that time, so he may have actually worked on this car!

Michael (center) met up with friends Bob (left) and Rob Ida. The Idas own one of the country's great custom and hot rod shops, which is located in New Jersey near the Englishtown drag strip.

—— 1968 CHEVY IMPALA CONVERTIBLE ——

This was a pretty cool set of wheels; a 427-cubic-inch, four-speed convertible that was absolutely loaded with accessories. Owner Gary Bossbach didn't want to sell, but…

"My intention was to restore the car when I retired in 2006," said the Bay City, Michigan, native. "But my life has changed, because now I go to Arizona regularly to work on a cattle ranch. Now I'm into RVs."

Gary said he'd sell the car for $25,000, which included a rebuilt engine and lots of N.O.S. parts. He was able to secure many genuine parts because he had worked in a small General Motors parts plant for 41 years.

"The car would cost $45,000 to $50,000 to restore, and could be worth $125,000 when finished," he said. "The original color is Butternut Yellow with white interior, so it will be really pretty."

This car has lots of potential; a rare 1968 Chevy convertible with a factory 427 engine and four-speed trans. Longtime owner Gary Bossbach of Michigan was selling it along with a truckload of N.O.S. parts.

—— VESPA CAR ——

Many folks have heard of and seen the small Italian scooters called Vespas. But most enthusiasts are surprised to learn that Vespa also made cars. The frontman for the rock band AC/DC, Brian Johnson, actually owns a Vespa car, and drives it around the paddock at the vintage car races where he competes.

Karl Krouch, who sells vintage automotive tools, was at Hershey selling this Vespa car for his landlord.

(above left) I did a couple of signing events for my book *50 Shades of Rust* while at Hershey: one at the *Hemming's Motor News* tent, and the other here, at the Society of Automotive Historians tent.

(above right) I've always wanted to check out the AACA Library to see if they had any information on Briggs Cunningham and the cars he built. This is a personal interest of mine.

(left) This was awkward; the bathroom at the library had an unusual design. The privy wasn't too private.

"My landlord has about 25 Lambrettas," said Karl. "This particular car is the Holy Grail of Vespa cars. It's a 1960." The company made 12,000 in 1958, and 7,000 in 1959, but, according to Karl, no production records exist for 1960 Vespas.

Karl was pretty well-versed in Vespas. He explained that the cars were powered by a two-cylinder, 2-cycle, air-cooled engine that put out a mighty 24 horsepower.

"There was no automotive production line in Italy like there had been for the scooters," he said. "So Vespa contracted with Piaggio in France to manufacture the cars."

That would explain the "Made in France" sticker in the engine compartment.

"This car was sold new in Boston to a woman in Maine. It was last driven in 1968, and garaged since."

Karl said the sale would include five new tires and new bumpers.

Karl Krouch was selling this Vespa car for his landlord. The 1960 model is complete but rusty. The price, however, would be an inexpensive way to get into the old car hobby.

Karl Krouch was selling this Vespa car for his landlord. The 1960 model is complete but rusty. The price, however, would be an inexpensive way to get into the old car hobby.

—— 1941 CHEVY PICKUP ——

Jonathan Ponulak makes his living by finding old cars and selling them. He has been doing it since his teens. He grew up in Summerville, New Jersey, and owns about 180 cars today.

"This truck had one owner," he said. "I bought it about one month ago. A friend called me and told me it was for sale on a front yard."

Jonathan said the seller was also selling a 1957 Chevy drag car. "The owner was in his 80s," he said. His father had bought it new in 1941. It was last driven in 1972 and has 72,000 on the odometer." Jonathan and his brother did a quick carb rebuild and a brake job. He said new wheel cylinders cost just $25 each.

This 1941 Chevy pickup was being sold by Jonathan Ponulak of Summerville, New Jersey. It was last driven in 1972, and has 72,000 miles on the odometer. It drew a lot of attention.

Michael fell in love with this Dodge two-door wagon, figuring it would be an ideal set of wheels for an automotive photographer to use when driving to a location.

Michael ran into old friend Mike Goodman, who worked at Honest Charlie's Speed Shop as a young man and now runs the operation.

He said finding old cars is getting tougher and tougher.

"The days of finding people who don't know the value of their cars are over," said Jonathan. "We're constantly looking for them, but if you stop at someone's house to inquire about a car, you better be prepared to buy it then."

— 1959 LINCOLN CONVERTIBLE —

John McClure was pissed.

He was sitting next to his massive '59 Lincoln convertible in the Hershey car corral, and he had just been told by the event organizers that his car had to be removed at the end of the day. The issue was that the car corral is for running, driving, and street-ready cars, and the organizers determined his Lincoln was a restoration project, and therefore needed to be parked in the flea market area.

John said to them, "But the car runs," but he couldn't change their minds.

John has been a Lincoln man for decades, and owns a business called The Lincoln Farm in Calvin, Pennsylvania. He has about 300 1949 to 1990 Lincolns in stock. And at one time, he had 300 Edsels, too.

Oh, and he also owns his great granddad's 1908 Brush Model B Runabout, which was manufactured in Detroit and sold for $550 new. Don't get excited, though, because the running, unrestored car is not for sale. But we're not here to talk about Brush Runabouts, we're here to talk about Lincolns.

Lincoln dealer John McClure was selling this 1959 Lincoln Continental convertible. The car ran well and only had 67,000 miles. It was surprisingly solid.

"I bought this '59 about two years ago from a body shop," he said. "It came as a package deal with two 1956 Lincoln Premier parts cars. He sent me photos, and I bought it. But I'm not going to get to restoring it, so it's for sale. It would be an ideal father-and-son project. It has 67,000 miles, and only 2,195 were built. I got it running, and it is sweet."

He told of how he hunts for cars.

"They are still out there in the most unexpected places," he said. "Many years ago, I was looking for 1930 Packard parts for a car I was restoring. A guy said to me, 'Why are you fooling around fixing up one sedan? I know where a whole barn is for sale that is loaded with cars for $100,000.' "So I told my banker about the opportunity, but he wouldn't loan me the money for the 10 or 12 classic cars. So I bought two of the cars and my friend bought the rest. We doubled our money.

"Realizing his mistake, my banker asked me to call him next time I heard about a collection like that for sale."

All in all, our searching for cars at Hershey was much less productive than searching for cars the old-fashioned way: driving through towns and neighborhoods, knocking on doors. Many of the cars we "found" at Hershey had been owned by their sellers for only a brief while, so they couldn't tell me much of a backstory about the car's earlier owners, or why the car went unused and was forgotten, etc. People out in the real world, who have years, or in some cases, generations, of experience with their cars, have much richer stories to tell.

So after three days at Hershey, it was time to head home in the morning. But only after another evening at Troeg's Brewery for more of their wonderful and funky German-themed food.

At the end of a long day, literally walking miles at Hershey, we found our way to Troeg's, one of our favorite micro-breweries.

The Hershey-based brewery makes beer on the premises and has incredible food, which I call "Funky German."

The Three Stooges, Michael, Brian, and I (left to right), getting a little punchy at Troeg's after nearly two weeks on the road.

THURSDAY, OCTOBER 9

>>>> **Ending Mileage: 24,088**

DAY

14

*O*ur original plan was to attend the AACA National Show at Hershey on Saturday. It is a fabulous show with hundreds of cars on display, all of which are the best in their class. If you've never been, I highly recommend it. The eclectic variety of vehicles—cars, trucks, motorcycles, and even restored mini-bikes—is amazing.

But we decided not to go to the show this year. The weather forecast was for an all-day rain, and we thought that rather than get rained on all day, we could head south and be home before evening.

To drive from the Hershey/Carlisle area to my house in Davidson, North Carolina, is a seven or eight hour trip if driven straight through. However, we had an appointment with a man who owned a huge MG collection back in Roanoke, Virginia. Remember, we had connected with a guy a week-and-a-half earlier,

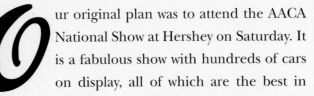

We stopped for lunch at my favorite restaurant when I'm traveling on I-81: Edelweiss German Restaurant off exit 213. Well worth a try if you get hungry and you're nearby.

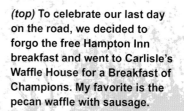

(top) To celebrate our last day on the road, we decided to forgo the free Hampton Inn breakfast and went to Carlisle's Waffle House for a Breakfast of Champions. My favorite is the pecan waffle with sausage.

(left) We decided to have a little fun when we checked out of our hotel room after our 14th day on the road; we took towels, pillows, and blankets to simulate a sleeping person on the cot. I wonder what the cleaning person thought when they walked in?

John Eldridge, who had more than 100 sports cars, mostly MGs, that he wanted to show us.

I called John, and he gave us directions to meet him in a Burger King parking lot. We met him there and followed him to his house, which was the only one in the neighborhood with MGBs in the driveway. We left the Woody and I climbed into a nice MGB that had plenty of patina, and Michael and Brian followed in the Flex.

This was the first time I'd ridden in an MGB in a long time, and it felt and sounded just right. That raspy, torquey little engine produced vibrations I hadn't experienced for at least 30 years, maybe more.

I bought a three-year-old 1969 MGB as a high school senior in 1972 and have always had a loyalty for the brand. I actually surprised my high school date by picking her up in the MG for the senior prom. Pat is now my wife. We've been married for, like, 100 years…

Anyway, a couple of paragraphs back, I introduced John as the owner of 100 sports cars, but he said he doesn't want to be known as a guy with 100 cars. "Let's just say I have 99 cars," he said. Actually, my tally is higher than that, but we'll stick to the 99 number.

John has been involved in MGs virtually all his adult life. In the mid-1960s, he moved from New York to the Roanoke, Virginia area, and, as a young man, followed his father as an employee of G.E. But, being a weekend sports car enthusiast and autocrosser in his Austin Healey Sprite, the lure of turning his hobby into a career was just too tempting. He resigned from G.E. and became an MG and Saab salesman at Foreign Car Specialists in Roanoke in 1968.

When we spoke to John Eldridge almost two weeks earlier, he told us he had about 100 British sports cars. First we visited one of his two fields of mostly MGBs. About 30 were resting here, used mostly for parts or future projects.

A year later, he became a 49 percent owner of the dealership and gave up sales for a service position. "I didn't like selling Saabs, so we hired a salesman," said John.

But his involvement with the dealership was short-lived; by 1970, his 49 percent ownership couldn't prevent him from being kicked out by his majority partner. So he hung up his own shingle. He opened Union Jack, Ltd., an MG service shop, just three blocks from his old dealership. He already had a good following, and he might just have been the cause of his old dealership folding three years later.

Call it sweet revenge.

Union Jack has been in business ever since, and still benefits today from John's early MG following.

"I've never advertised," said John. "It's all been word of mouth. It's been very steady all these years. In fact, lately, I'm swamped!"

He said much of his business comes from mentions on the Web. "Once I got a call from a woman who wanted to speak to Jack," he said. "Google had listed my business's name as Jack Union."

Anyway, this man has a lot of MGs. We followed him to field #1, which is out in the country. There were more than 30 MGs sitting in the grass. These cars were either only good for parts cars, or perhaps restoration or racing projects.

He has another field, which we did not visit because it was quite a distance out of town, but he mentioned that a similar number of MGs were sitting there as well.

At this point, John turned the MG driving chores over to me. This brought back wonderful memories and confirmed to me that these cars are reliable enough to be fun, daily drivers.

A lonely MGA roadster sits under a shed roof, with a lineup of its younger relatives in the background.

Next, John brought us to his shop, Union Jack, Ltd. This is where John comes every day to repair and restore MGs for his customers. A couple of restoration projects were inside.

MG repair and restoration have been John Eldridge's life for half a century. John will repair or restore your MG, or sell you any of the *99* he owns.

(top) Inside the nicely cluttered shop were mostly MGBs, but here and there were other cars, such as this MGTF that is undergoing a restoration.

(above) Another is this MGTD, which seems to have taken up root in the corner under a stack of cardboard boxes.

Finally, John brought us to his storage barn. This is where he keeps the best cars, including some like-new MGs and the best restoration projects.

Next, we traveled to his shop, which is in downtown Roanoke. The building was jammed with lots of parts and probably eight or ten cars that were either being serviced or restored. "I'd say 60 to 70 percent of my business is servicing MGs, and the rest is restoration work," he said.

Finally we drove to a very large dairy barn that John rents to store his best cars. This barn is ideal for car storage; large, well lit, and with a concrete floor.

Inside were another 30 or so cars; again, mostly MGs. Many were solid, original examples, and others were in the process of being restored. One was an extremely low mileage 1980, which was in showroom condition. Sprinkled among the MGs were the occasional Triumph (TR6, Spitfire) and Austin Healey (3000, Sprite).

I asked John how he buys his cars.

"To me, it's no different from trading stock," he said. "I used to buy old MGs for $100, but now I'll pay scrap value. If a 3,000-pound car is shredded, the scrap yard will pay $200. I will also pay $200, but I am willing to pay extra for a part like a new carburetor or a new gas tank that might be in the car."

John also restores cars on spec. This was an intriguing idea to me. If a customer wants, say, a 1967 MGB, John will build it in the color the customer choses. It will include a rebuilt engine, trans, rear end, hydraulics, electrical system and wiring

Rows of rust-free MGs (and the Austin Healey Sprite in the foreground) rest in the dry building.

harness, new interior, tires, etc. On top of that, the customer can choose options such as wire wheels, leather interior, or a canvas top. Functionally a new car, John might charge $14,000 or so for it, depending on the number of upgrades. This is cheaper than a new Kia sedan. I think it makes an ideal alternative to a cheap, new car, and it's certainly more fun on weekends.

In the middle of many MGBs was this wonderful Austin Healey Bugeye Sprite, which would make a terrific project for someone.

"Keeping MGs on the road is the main thing," he said. "And I'll do that by either selling parts or cars."

And with that, we were back on the road for home. A fruitful two weeks, wouldn't you say?

Some of the cars in John's field are definitely worthy of restoration, but others, like this one, are more suitable as yard sculpture.

The three of us arrive at my house, two weeks after leaving. Brian, Michael, and I are surrounded by some of the contents of the two vehicles: luggage, photography equipment, tools, and some of the parts we purchased in Hershey. The Barn Find Road Trip was a resounding success! I've just got one question—where to next?

— BARN FIND ROAD TRIP BEST OF... —

BEST FOOD
DEVON'S RESTAURANT (SEAFOOD)
HERSHEY, PA

BEST PUB FOOD
TROEG'S BREWERY
HERSHEY, PA

BEST BARMAID
MOLLY HATCHETT
MOUNTAIN JAX, MARTINSVILLE, VA

BEST RESTAURANT VIEW
FRONT PORCH RESTAURANT
SENECA ROCKS, WV

BEST PIE
ANTIQUE ENGINE SHOW, MD

BEST BREAKFAST
WAFFLE HOUSE
CARLISLE, PA

BEST ICE CREAM
BAUGHER'S RESTAURANT
AND ICE CREAM
WESTMINSTER, MD

BEST BEER
WASENA CITY TAP ROOM
ROANOKE, VA

BEST PIZZA
WATERSTONE FIRE ROASTED PIZZA
LYNCHBURG, VA

BEST FOOD TRUCK
MACAROLLIN
HERSHEY, PA

BEST EVENT FOOD
SHERRIE'S CRAB CAKES
HERSHEY, PA

— OTHER —

BEST BUILDING (TIE)
OLD FORD DEALERSHIP
SENECA ROCKS, WV
BRUCE ELDER'S OLD FORD DEALERSHIP
STAUNTON, VA

BEST ROAD
HIGHWAY 8 TOWARD HIGHWAY 57 FROM
REINER TO WOOLWINE, VA

CARS WE'D MOST LIKE TO OWN
FROM OUR DISCOVERIES
BRIAN—1966 LINCOLN CONTINENTAL
MICHAEL—1948 CHEVROLET SEDAN
DELIVERY (HERSHEY)
TOM—1958 FUELLY CORVETTE

BEST ROAD NAME–TIE
FRIED MEAT RIDGE ROAD
BURLINGTON, WV
DIRTY FOOT ROAD
SHORT GAP, WV

MOST INTERESTING EVENT
ANTIQUE ENGINE SHOW, MD

BEST EQUIPMENT FIND
1940 SEAGRAVES HOOK &
LADDER FIRETRUCK
ROANOKE, VA

Top 10 Rules of Barn-Find Hunting

1. Always Search on the Wrong Side of Town

We made a point of always locating the commercial side of the tracks when we arrived in a new town. These are areas that are more populated by auto repair and body shops. And, potentially, houses where cars are more visible. To go to the "right" side of town, which is more likely to be populated by law offices or insurance agencies, will probably not yield many barn-find vehicles. Homes on the right side of the tracks might actually have old cars, but more than likely they will be stored inside garages and difficult to see.

2. You Can Go Home Again

If you knew of older car guys when you were a kid in your hometown, go back and check in on them today. Even if it's been decades, and you live on the other side of the country, scan through your old neighborhood next time you're home for the holidays or attending a class reunion. Several years ago I purchased a rare Abarth coupe by going past a house where I remembered a bunch of neat sports cars when I passed on the school bus. And a friend told me he visited his high school class reunion and discovered the 1932 Ford roadster he saw as a student, still hibernating in a garage. He was able to buy it.

3. Tour Residential Areas on Weekends

And commercial districts on weekdays. Think about it: if you are a homeowner, you ignore your house and garden during the week, but you make up for it on the weekends. Those are the days you trim the hedges, clean the gutters, and wash the cars. And those activities are usually done with the garage door open. This is a barn-finder's fantasy; a time when hidden vehicles are temporarily exposed to sunlight. And to your eyes.

On the other hand, most auto-related businesses are open during the week but closed Saturday and Sunday. So that body shop or used car dealer—with all the old cars on the back row—is better approached Monday through Friday. Of course, sometimes these formulas don't always work, but after 14 days on the road, we've found it to be pretty true.

4. Become Friends

With people who can go onto private property legally. Folks like policemen, landscapers, and UPS and Fed Ex delivery people. These folks can see far beyond what you can see from the road. And they can look behind buildings and peek into garage windows. I once owned a barn-find Cobra that was discovered by a propane-gas deliveryman. Through a window, he saw a sports car shape under a cover inside the garage that he thought was a Triumph or an MG. It turned out to be the 149th Cobra ever manufactured.

5. Embrace Dead Ends

These are the roads less traveled. Think about it: when you get the end of a dead-end street, you have to make an awkward U-turn to reverse direction. People avoid these roads like the

continued on next page

continued from previous page

plague. So guess what—the old cars that are parked in yards on those roads are only seen by a small number of people. In this book, we were told of a Plymouth Superbird that was on a dead-end street off an interstate exit. Nobody would go down that road unless they had a reason. We had a reason and found not a Superbird, but a Dodge Super Bee that was purchased new by Charles Grant. Great find and great story.

6. Write Letters

To the owners of old cars who are not interested in selling. Sometimes a nice letter is a lasting reminder about the nice fellow who came to your door and asked about the Duesenberg. Additionally, I have heard time and time again that if an elderly owner is diseased or becomes disabled, relatives will often go through their letters and effects. They are most likely unsure what to do with the vehicles that were in their loved one's possession, so finding your letter might just begin a dialogue that would end in you being offered the car. I've heard of it happening many times.

7. Hunt in the Winter

When the leaves are off the trees. This plan doesn't work so well if you live in Phoenix, but if you live in New England, your eyesight will double in the winter because all those leaves won't be blocking your view.

8. Talk to the Old Timers

This is a tip I got from Jay Leno. He goes to a city or town and hunts down the old timers; old auto or motorcycle mechanics, auto parts store countermen, even lawn mower repairmen. His feeling is that these people have lived in the town for a long, long time, and they are mechanically inclined. They might very well remember "Old Joe, who used to fool around with Studebakers before he died. There's still a building filled with his cars…," that type of thing.

9. Befriend a Lawyer

Lawyers often settle estates, handle bankruptcies, and know "people's private business" that is not meant to go public. If you ask lawyers to keep you in mind in the event that interesting old cars need to be liquidated, you might just score an interesting treasure.

10. Google Earth, Ultralight, or Drone

I hadn't actually done this until this road trip, but, I mean, why not? If you suspect cars may be hidden out of sight behind a building or landscaping, how about searching from above? We tried this on our first day, discovering Snowball Bishop's field of 60 or so old Fords via Google Earth. I once heard from a Blimp pilot who would hover low over interesting farms when commuting back and forth along the East Coast, looking for cars. Now with drones available for less than $1,000, you can attach your GoPro camera and take off for the heavens!

Epilogue

It was an amazing two weeks. Was it long? Yes, a long time away from home-cooked meals, a long time to be driving nonstop from sunrise to sunset, and a long time to share a hotel room with two snoring guys. But we met amazing people, saw great scenery, and found an incredible number of cars.

They are still out there!

When my publisher, Zack Miller, agreed to produce this book, he wondered if we could find as many as 100 cars. It was hard to predict. I mean, if we were lucky, yes, we could probably find that many cars. Who knew until we actually hit the road?

Well, through some good luck, asking the right questions, and keeping our eyes peeled, we found more than ten times that amount! The final tally was 1,558 cars, trucks, motorcycles, and one fire truck!

Amazing. Did we luck out? Did we just pick the four correct states?

Yes, I think that was partly the case. Certainly, the four states we covered—Virginia, West Virginia, Maryland, and Pennsylvania—have large amounts of rural countryside, yet also have densely packed urban areas. We never had to spend too much time traveling between towns, or even states.

But I believe that we would be successful in any other four states, as well. On the other hand, it would be hard to find such a large volume of cars in a state like, say, Montana or North Dakota, simply because the population density is so much smaller and the urban centers are much farther apart. If we used the same techniques for searching for old cars in other states, I think folks would be surprised at the large number of interesting vehicles we'd find. It might just take a little longer.

The GPS tells me that the drive from my house to Hershey and back is 950 miles. However, we drove a route that had us cover 2,282 miles. A worthy detour, I would say.

Would I do it again? Would I travel with two other guys, share hotel rooms, and drive all day in search of forgotten relics? In a heartbeat. In fact, if this book sells well enough, maybe Zack will give us another shot at searching for cars in four *different* states. Or 50 states!

50 States of Rust…

What do you think? What states would you recommend? Would you buy another book like this?

Brian, Michael, and I had a blast living out this fantasy. It's been a pleasure writing this for you. I hope you enjoyed the results.

Tom Cotter

Index